READER'S
COMPANION
TO THE
BIBLE

Reader's

Companion

to the

Bible

by RALPH D. HEIM

FORTRESS PRESS • Philadelphia

To
Marianna and John
with love

Biblical quotations from the Revised Standard Version Common Bible,
copyright © 1973 by the Division of Christian Education of the
National Council of the Churches of Christ in the U.S.A., are used
by permission.

COPYRIGHT © 1975 BY FORTRESS PRESS
All rights reserved. No part of this publication may be reproduced,
stored in a retrieval system, or transmitted in any form or by any
means, electronic, mechanical, photocopying, recording, or otherwise, without the prior permission of the copyright owner.

Library of Congress Catalog Card Number 74-26329
ISBN 0-8006-1090-3

4637A75   Printed in U.S.A.   1-1090

Contents

NEW TESTAMENT

Preface: About This Book and Its Uses

Reader's Companion to the Bible is meant to help any person consult, read, or study the Bible with more understanding, satisfaction, and help for day-to-day living. It can help meet the needs of people in the churches and even assist students in various types of schools who are preparing or reviewing for a course.

More generally, it will be of interest to persons who, having more time or sense of need, may wish to start regular use of the Bible in a more thorough and meaningful way. They may have said to themselves, "At last I am going to get better acquainted with my Bible"—and then recognized that they need help.

To these and to others *Reader's Companion* will be:

1. An interpreter to point out the most important, interesting, and transforming passages, lend them a sense of reality, and give them clearer meaning.
2. A tutor on what is now widely considered correct in biblical history, literature, and teaching.
3. A guide to help discover materials for special needs.

General articles will throw light on the nature of the Bible as a whole and on how to use its several forms of literature. Short treatments will introduce the 66 books, one by one, describing their nature and suggesting their particular values. Lists of selected readings will help a reader find the key passages of each book, understand its teachings more exactly, and utilize its messages more readily. A final section lists 300 compelling human concerns and cites biblical passages which can be helpful in relation to them.

All these materials together should lead the reader to meet:

1. The greatest events, most noteworthy passages, and loveliest beauty spots in the Bible.
2. The major facts of biblical history and literature but also the great calls to action and challenges to a new way of life.

3. The outstanding personalities, appearing more real and with their teachings more inviting.
4. The most significant insights and revelations, the clearest declarations of God's nature and will for man, and especially the salvation message.

There is good reason to hope that one who uses this book in connection with his Bible reading and study will not only learn new facts concerning biblical matters. More important, he or she will experience greater faith in God, closer fellowship with Jesus Christ, and a more blessed daily walk among God's people.

Introduction: The Word of Life for the Whole of Life

The Bible is the vital record of man's discoveries concerning what God has made known about his nature and his will for mankind's blessing. It is most often called Word of God and it does bear a message from God about the relationships of humanity with him and among themselves.

WORD OF LIFE

The Bible may also be called Word of Life. It came from the life of God through human life into written form to become life again in those who let its writing have its way with them. Through the Bible there is to be more life, abundant life, eternal life.

These ancient writers say that God is, God loves, God expects, God helps, God saves; therefore live as his children, trusting him and working at his tasks. The disobedient must expect disaster, although there is forgiveness for those who repent; the faithful will not escape trouble, but God will care for them graciously.

Those men of God had had experiences in which God met and helped them. There they gained this knowledge that they put into their writing. Now the knowledge can be brought into similar situations of modern persons so that these, too, can meet God and have his help. The Bible is a storehouse of materials that gives its readers examples of, and moving statements about, the right and wrong among the things they feel, think, and do. It demonstrates the rewards and penalties of various human acts. It makes available what God had done and is willing to do for his people. It stirs them and lends them power to act according to his purposes for them.

FOR ALL LIFE

The Bible is Word of Life for the whole of life. It is for all people: red, white, black, yellow, or brown speaking 1500 languages and spanning the globe. It speaks to every age and condition: child, youth, adult—of high and low degree, rich and poor, healthy and sick, strong and weak. As it came by way of all sorts of men and women it is for farmers, fishermen, artisans, merchants, housewives, rulers, parents, priests, and teachers. Tested by such persons in the many centuries, it fits any future including our own troublous, changing times. The Bible is, indeed, the universal Word of Life—revelation that is to become living word in and through all persons who know it.

USING THE WORD OF LIFE

A hundred men and women once wrote about how they were using their Bibles and what this use meant for them. A favorite testimonial about the worth of what they were doing was to say they wanted to "give it more time." Essentially, three things were happening among these people:

They were reading with study. Many of the hundred were seeking more knowledge about the Book and its meaning. They participated in classes but also engaged in self-study. Book studies were commended by some who had undertaken them regularly. Many said helps were needed for the best results: guides like this, modern versions, a concordance, a harmony of the Gospels, commentaries which church and city libraries provide or can be purchased for oneself. Some readers treasure a Bible worn by years of study and heavily marked with notes on the most interesting, beautiful, and meaningful passages.

They were reading in private worship. Most of those hundred readers put their emphasis, as one said, on "keeping contact with the unseen world." Their Bible time was in the morning, at mealtime, or on retiring. Many were reading with a devotional manual or other list of suggestions. Those who were using only the Bible might be reading ten verses or a chapter a day, going through the whole Book of favorite books and chapters. Others paid attention to their mood or need at the moment.

They were finding help for their living. It is possible to list a few of the specific benefits mentioned: have help to be more kind and to overcome temptation; have a source of peace, power, and comfort; have "courage for the day and strength to endure"; keep fellowship with Jesus Christ. Some appreciated the Bible's inspiring calls to action in the service of God and man. One who had been reading his Bible through a long life testified: "The more often you read a passage the more help you have for faithful living."

LIVING THE WORD OF LIFE

The really vital necessity in using the Bible is to live by it. The word must be allowed to yield wise understanding, sound belief, and appropriate action. One who uses the Bible with earnest purpose and eager expectation will be wise to ask these questions as he reads:

What was the author in his time and way trying to teach through these words?

What is he saying about God? Man? Morals and religion? Right and abundant living?

How would he like to inform me? Stir me? Guide me? Help me?

What now do I believe and intend to do?

To be remembered throughout: The inscripturated Word of Life is to become life in the flesh.

OLD
TESTAMENT

The Old Testament People, History, and Literature

We know this library of 66 books that we call the Bible as two testaments: Old Testament with 39 books; New Testament with 27. Testament means "covenant," a solemn agreement concerning the relationships of God and his people—what each will do. According to the Old Testament the people may expect God's steadfast love and righteous judgment; God may expect faithful devotion and service.

We know the Old Testament people as Hebrews by race, usually called Israelites or children of Israel—another name for Jacob —and Jews. Their history for nearly 2000 years occurred in four eras:

1. Patriarchs (beginning about 1900 B.C.). The story opens with a great pioneer, Abraham. Coming from Ur, some 500 miles east of present Jerusalem, he emigrated with his father northwest to Haran. There he received a call to go southwest to Canaan, now Israel. Abraham was assured that God would make him father of a great nation; also that by him (Genesis 12:3) . . . *all the families of the earth shall bless themselves.* For this purpose his nation would be God's "chosen people." The Old Testament tells its readers next about Abraham's family until a great-grandson, Joseph, moves the family into Egypt about 1700 B.C.

2. Moses, Joshua, Judges (beginning about 1350 B.C.). After several centuries of the Hebrew's residence in Egypt, Moses, their favorite hero, was born. Because a hostile Egyptian ruler was oppressing them, Moses led them back to the borders of the old homeland. Under Joshua they entered, conquered, and settled there. For some two centuries following, judges appeared in national crises to save one tribe or another from an enemy.

3. Kings (about 1020–587 B.C.). Saul, first king, was anointed about 1020. David followed, 1000–961; then Solomon reigned, 961–922. After him a Northern Kingdom lasted until its ten tribes were led away by the Assyrians about 721. A Southern

Kingdom ended with the fall of Jerusalem, 587; then its two deported tribes had to live for a half century in Babylonian exile.

4. *The exile to the Christian era.* In 538 B.C., Cyrus of Persia, who had conquered Babylon, decreed that Jews who chose might return to Jerusalem. Some did in 536, and their descendants lived through successive Persian, Greek, Egyptian, and Syrian occupations. They regained a measure of independence about 160 but Romans conquered the area in 63 and were ruling there when Christ came. (A touching bit of nonbiblical history, only since A.D. 1948 have the Jews been a nation again.)

Old Testament books of history, law, poetry, wisdom, and prophecy had their origins, of course, with events they report and storytellers who kept alive the accounts. Yet the time came when authors wrote what are now fragments in existing records. Then others combined bits of the older writing with their own to make many of the books we have. There are also the more original works of poets, sages, prophets, and priests who wrote them in their appropriate ways. Amos was the first book to be completed, about 750 B.C.; Daniel the last, not long before 150 B.C.

After a book had been written the next step was to copy and recopy it. Another step was canonization. Along with the present Old Testament books similar ones were produced. The particular 39 that had proved most helpful were canonized, declared the sacred scriptures of the Hebrews, about A.D. 100. Translations from the Hebrew into other languages began early. The first English translation—both testaments handwritten—was made by John Wycliffe, A.D. 1380.

Books of History and Law

There are seventeen books in the historical and legal section of the Old Testament. This section begins with Genesis and ends with Esther.

Many of the historical books, which include also biographical books and others, were completed by that process called compilation in which authors and editors joined selections from former writing with their own work, weaving it all together like strands of a rope. Scholars speak of four principal sources:

"J" a history which came out of Judah about 950 B.C.

"E" a similar work by Ephraimites of the North, 750 B.C.

"D" by Deuteronomic, second law, writers about 650 B.C.

"P" by priestly writers in Babylon about 550 B.C.

Roughly the Pentateuch, Genesis through Deuteronomy, includes these in combinations completed in Babylon by 500 B.C. and seems to have appeared in Jerusalem somewhat after 450 B.C.

It is thought that Joshua, Judges, First and Second Samuel, and First and Second Kings also were completed in Babylon before 500 B.C. Four more historical works appeared about 400 B.C.: First and Second Chronicles, Ezra, and Nehemiah. Some of these mention older books used as sources.

Recognizing compilation in the origin of certain biblical books is important when using them. We may be reading in the same book from one author and then another. This is one reason we have repetitions that sometimes seem to be contradictory. Actually it is our good fortune to have a variety of witnesses to give us a broader view, as in the two accounts of creation.

All this Old Testament historical literature is especially valuable for the great biographies that can challenge, beckon, warn, and move even twentieth-century Christians. In general, Old Testament history illumines the past and present while it gives glimpses into the future. Above all else it discloses God's unceasing purpose. He and his people are building a kingdom of righteousness and love that is to be breaking into all other kingdoms. The record can elicit from modern persons patriotic action for that kingdom just as other history is used in public education to develop loyal citizens for a nation and United Nations.

The legal literature of the Old Testament is included in Exodus, Leviticus, Deuteronomy, and other books. It is represented in the Christian community chiefly by the Ten Commandments. Yet these books of law contain additional material for regulating almost every facet of Hebrew life. Statutes regarding tabernacle and temple, sacrifice, sabbath, and festival are most prominent. Numerous laws deal with personal hygiene, health, and the use or avoidance of various foods. Correct communal relationships for neighbor and slave, the sick and injured, strong and weak, enemy and ally are stressed. Among the principal legal portions to be mentioned as they appear in the books that include them are the Covenant Code, Deuteronomic Code, Holiness Code, and Ezekiel's Code.

This material is not utterly outgrown. Here we meet the basis for the present day law and moral and religious practices ingrained in Western culture. It can foster interracial and interfaith understanding. Knowing it is essential for full understanding of New Testament teaching in the Gospels and the controversy about legalism and freedom which Paul reports in his epistles. We could wish that some provisions were operative today. Vastly important for its proper interpretation, though, this law changed as the Hebrew nation developed. Further, the New Testament moves it to higher ground in, for example, the Sermon on the Mount.

What particular teaching values do these books of history and law provide? Book by book we shall see. In general, they will provide light and power for those who seek answers to such questions as these:

What has God done; what is he doing; what will he do?
Who and where are we, how did we get here, in this condition?
What ought we do as individuals and society?
How can we arrive at the higher goals of life?

GENESIS
In the beginning God . . . (1:1a)

Where did everything come from? Mankind keeps wondering. When we confess our Apostles' Creed we say, "I believe in God the Father Almighty, maker of heaven and earth." The writers of Genesis, like ourselves, believed that God is the powerful Father, creative source of all that exists and provident caretaker of it. Things, including man, are not accidents of chance but acts of God's love, with man as his most cherished work.

So it was written in what has become the first book we meet

in our Bibles. While half the other Old Testament books had been completed before it, Genesis comes first, fittingly because here is what Hebrew writers, several hundreds of years before Christ, believed God had given them to teach about beginnings.

Genesis opens, naturally, with the beginnings of man and all he can see around him; next it deals with origins of sin, death, and other features of human existence. The rest of the first eleven chapters report a flood and new beginning. Already man's fitful sinfulness and faithfulness, along with God's enduring justice and grace, have been brilliantly highlighted.

Chapter 3, on what we call the temptation and fall, has long received special attention. It is an example of the symbolic writing, like parable and poetry, that the Bible uses so often to say what is best taught in something more than bare fact and common language. It is a precious body of teaching about the fallingness of all God's children and their recovery by the savingness of a God who visits his erring children and seeks what the New Testament describes as lost sheep.

Chapters 12 through 36 recount the beginnings of a special family for that great purpose of being a blessing to . . . *all the families of the earth* . . . (12:3). Believers consider themselves participants in that purpose and heirs to the promise of blessing God made to that family. The book concludes with fourteen chapters about Joseph and his family. The grandest story in all Genesis is told about Joseph and his brothers (see the selected reading 42:1–45:15).

Genesis, like all other books in the Bible, was written for moral and religious purposes. The authors are not teaching about science but about the life of man with God.

SELECTED READINGS

God creates and provides for his world and his people   1:1–2:4a
This book of beginnings opens with two Hebrew stories to say that God made everything, including man and woman *in his image*. This first was written by priests exiled in Babylon about 500 B.C. The other (2:4b–24) comes from historians of about 950 B.C.

Adam and Eve disobey God   3:1–24

This account of the origin of sin is a portrayal of sin's nature at any time and, more important, of God's everlasting grace with justice.

God sends a flood; a new beginning follows   6:5–9:17

Priestly compilers have mingled two accounts of the event which teaches that God is just, but also loving.

Abraham (Abram in the Common Bible) has a call at Haran, receives a mission and promise; moves to Canaan   12:1–9

This is the beginning of the family through which Christ came. Now God has a "chosen people" to accomplish his purpose of blessing mankind. The date is about 1900 B.C.

Abraham and Lot divide the land of Canaan   13:2–13

The first "Lot's choice"; greed has drastic consequences.

Abraham's and Sarah's son Isaac is spared from sacrifice   22:1–14
Isaac and Rebekah wed; have twin sons Esau and Jacob   24:1–67

Esau will father the Edomites, Jacob the Israelites.

The quiet one, Jacob, wins sportsman Esau's birthright   25:27–34

A Hebrew oldest son would become head of the family at his father's death. That birthright belongs to Esau, born first.

Crafty Jacob steals Esau's blessing; Esau vows vengeance   27:1–45

For ancient Hebrews a dying father's blessing was a powerful prayer for the one blessed. A blot on motherhood, Jacob's mother, partial to him, helps him deceive his father.

Jacob, fleeing Esau's fury, dreams and vows at Bethel   28:10–22

Bethel means "house of God." Weary, lonely, or guilty persons may meet God unexpectedly; they rightly respond in dedication.

Jacob lives with uncle Laban; marries Leah and Rachel   29:1–30
Brothers Jacob and Esau meet again and are reconciled   32:3–33:14
Joseph and eleven brothers live in Canaan   37:1–36

Joseph, favorite son, gets a *long robe with sleeves* (formerly called "coat of many colors"); dreams of ruling his brothers.

Joseph's stay in Egypt 42:1–45:15

Joseph becomes Egypt's food administrator; the brothers come to him for food. Joseph secretly knows them. When they come again he tests their honor by having a cup hidden in a bag of grain but seemingly stolen by Benjamin. When Judah nobly offers to be a slave to pay Benjamin's penalty, Joseph reveals his identity.

Jacob enters Goshen with the brothers and families 45:16–46:7
Jacob dies; Joseph has forgiven his brothers 50:15–21

There is no further biblical record until Moses.

EXODUS

. . . let my people go . . . (5:1)

Exodus is the first book of a four-volume biography of Moses. The Hebrews rightly regarded this hero so highly that they used also Leviticus, Numbers, and Deuteronomy for the story of his life and work. He does tower over all other early Old Testament personalities as he leads the Hebrews in their escape from Egypt, brings down the law from Sinai, and shepherds his people to the gates of their Promised Land.

Perhaps 400 years have passed since the happier days of Joseph. His descendants are held in bitter slavery under Egyptian taskmasters. Just now newborn male children are being drowned in the Nile in order to limit the Hebrew population.

Moses' family saved their baby boy in the way we learned as children. But Moses, grown to manhood, kills an Egyptian who was beating a Hebrew. Discovered, he flees to Midian on the Sinai Peninsula, now in Saudi Arabia, where he will later guide the refugee Israelites. There he envisions a burning bush from which the Lord summons him to lead his people out of Egypt.

The Pharaoh steadfastly refused permission for the Hebrew emigration. Plagues forced his consent, but even then he changed his mind and pursued the departing company with his army. Surviving this hazard and others, the people reached Mt. Sinai.

There the Ten Commandments were proclaimed. These verses

of Exodus 20:1–17 are the most frequently used passage of the Old Testament. It is right to stress the Ten; no civilization could endure without observing them. However, the Sermon on the Mount is incomparably the more important body of standards for character and conduct. The Ten need to be "fulfilled." As instances, the three that forbid killing, adultery, and theft can be put into these positive forms instead of the negative ones:

Work for the fuller life of self and others.

Foster chastity in thought, word, and deed.

Assist a neighbor to increase and improve his property.

SELECTED READINGS

Jacob's descendants are oppressed in Egypt   1:8–16

The time is about 1350 B.C. Jacob's family had been welcomed to Egypt in the days of Joseph but now the Egyptians have reduced the Hebrews to slave labor and are using infanticide to keep their numbers within bounds. Happily, a deliverer is about to arise.

A princess rescues Moses from the Nile and adopts him   2:1–10
After a murder, Moses flees into the Arabian Peninsula   2:11–22
Moses in Midian accepts God's call from a burning bush   3:1–4:17

He is to lead the Israelites back to Palestine. Aaron will help him; God will do wonders.

Following plagues, Israel celebrates the first Passover   12:1–32

Jews celebrate their deliverance annually. Christians remember that Christ was crucified at Passover time.

Moses leads the Israelites across the Red Sea   13:17–14:30

There is a further description in Chapter 15, a later poem.

God provides as the people "murmur" for food and water   16:1–36
Moses and Israel reach Mount Sinai (also called Horeb)   19:1–25

There is a Christian chapel now on the traditional mount.

Moses brings down the Ten Commandments from the mount 20:1–17

Other accounts are in Exodus 34(J) and Deuteronomy 5(D).

The Covenant Code, oldest of several such codes   20:22–23:33
A body of laws from about 750 B.C. Later ones are more humane.

The people are to have an ark   25:1–40
A lavishly ornamented center for worship containing sacred relics and symbolizing the presence of God.

Israel builds a tabernacle   35:1–40:38
The people have a tent for worship services in their wanderings.

LEVITICUS
. . . be holy for I am holy. (11:44)

This book has its name because it was chiefly a manual on the duties of Hebrew priests or Levites, members of the tribe of Levi, who were to lead worship. Yet it also contains minute regulations for much personal and group conduct. Here we have the Holiness Code so-called because, as God's holiness is proclaimed, the holiness of his people is commanded.

Materials on sacrifices, rituals, uncleanness and purification, vows and tithes will have little more than historical value for modern readers. Yet Leviticus has its gems of spiritual insight. It was from this book that Jesus was quoting when he said (19:18), *you shall love your neighbor as yourself.*

Too, we have in 24:17–21 the kind of lesser law to which Jesus referred in the Sermon on the Mount. In Matthew 5:38–42 there are beautiful examples of the manner in which he raised that ancient law to nobler heights. Grievous mistakes are made by persons who quote and foster Old Testament prescriptions instead of the higher ideals of Jesus.

One of our nation's shrines of liberty is the room in which the Liberty Bell is housed. Thousands come there weekly and see around the bell's rim the words, according to the King James Version: Proclaim Liberty Throughout All the Land unto All the Inhabitants Thereof. The words are from Leviticus 25:10, dealing with sabbatical years. After seven of these seventh years there was to be a jubilee year in which every person must be freed from bondage.

Scholars have concluded that Leviticus was completed in Babylon and brought to Jerusalem not long after 450 B.C. It may be the law which, we shall see, Ezra and Nehemiah introduced to the people there. While Leviticus may be the least read of all biblical books, it can still be an eloquent reminder that a holy God impels his people to be holy sons and daughters.

SELECTED READINGS

The sacrifice of burnt-offering   1:1–17
Chapters 1 through 7 provide also for making other sacrifices.

Laws of diet   11:1–47
Essentials of ethical conduct   19:1–37
A sample of the Holiness Code with 19:18 on love for neighbor.

The "life for life" law   24:17–21
Vengeful retaliation, allowed in Genesis 4:23, 24, is limited here, and even this "lex talionis" (law of talons) is transcended by Jesus in the Sermon on the Mount. Like this instance all law should be developing into better law.

Sabbath year and year of jubilee   25:1–55

NUMBERS

The Lord bless you . . . keep you . . .give you peace.
(6:24-26)

This fourth book of the Bible with the unpromising title gets its names from two "numberings" of the Israelites during their years in the wilderness of the Sinai Peninsula. The first census (Chapters 1 through 4) was taken not long after the Exodus and the second (Chapter 26) near the end of the wandering.

The book's Hebrew name, which means "In the Wilderness," is more fitting for it suggests better the time, place, and nature of the content. Only five chapters deal with the numberings, thirty-one cover the people's trials as they wander between Egypt and Canaan. A quantity of law is interwoven.

At first the Hebrews are encamped near Sinai where the Ten

Commandments are given them. After two years Moses leads them to Kadesh-Barnea, a hundred miles south of Jerusalem. There a decisive event takes place. Twelve spies, sent out to reconnoiter, return with glowing reports about the country and its produce. Yet only two, Caleb and Joshua, favor immediate advance to enter the land and conquer the tribes already there. The other ten and the people themselves are afraid to make the venture. So all have to remain a generation at Kadesh while hardier souls with greater faith grow up.

A final section of the book (Chapters 20 through 36) tells about the journey from Kadesh to the plains of Moab, just east of the Dead Sea. Now the new generation is ready for the conquest and occupation. But their beloved Moses can go no farther. With Joshua as their new leader they will cross Jordan and in time win back the ancient fatherland.

Life in the Hebrew camp at Kadesh-Barnea must have been a bitter struggle just to survive. Yet this hard experience built the men and women who could endure the stress and strain to come. As it would be said in an Epistle to the Hebrews (12:11) a dozen centuries later, *For the moment all discipline seems painful rather than pleasant; later it yields the pleasant fruit of righteousness to those who have been trained by it.*

SELECTED READINGS

Moses is to take a census   1:1–19
Moses receives the Aaronic benediction   6:22–27

In the midst of preparations for the advance, God gives this blessing to be used then by Aaron and his sons, now by us.

Moses leads his people from Sinai to Kadesh   10:11–36
Twelve spies reconnoiter Canaan and report   13:1–14:10a

The fearful people must remain "forty years" at Kadesh.

Moses and Israel encamp on the plains of Moab   22:1

At last they are on the way, poised for conquest at the gates of their future home.

| Moses takes a second census | 26:1-65 |
| Moses commissions Joshua as his successor | 27:12-23 |

Deuteronomy will report Moses' death and burial.

DEUTERONOMY
Hear, O Israel . . . (6:4a)

The strange name of this book means "second lawgiving." As an instance of the title's fitness, we have here a second listing of the Ten Commandments; the book also contains what is called the Deuteronomic Code (Chapters 12–26, 28). The high quality of Deuteronomy's teachings is attested by the fact that it seems to have been a favorite with Jesus. From it he quoted (6:4): *you shall love the Lord your God with all your heart, and with all your soul, and with all your might.*

The authors open with the Israelites about to enter the Promised Land; they close with Moses' death and burial in the hills of Moab to the East. As their way to present the material, the aged leader gives three orations: 1:6–4:40; 5:1–26:19 and 28:1–68; 29:2–30:20. In these he recounts their recent history and reviews the laws that are to govern the people. He also charges the new leader Joshua to be *strong and of good courage* and admonishes his followers to remember God's loving care for them and to serve him faithfully.

Many scholars believe that this book—at least part of it—is the *book of the law* that was discovered (Second Chronicles 34:15) during the reign of Josiah, King of Judah, 640–609. The book was appearing about 620 although probably it was written about 650 B.C. When Josiah's grandfather Manasseh sat on the throne of Judah—a king as wicked as Josiah would be noble—he harassed the prophets but they, hopeful as usual, looked forward to a better day. They even prepared for it by writing this book with a new code of laws for the nation at that future time. Then they stored it where it would be "found." When Josiah became king he renovated the temple that had fallen into disrepair during previous reigns. Then workmen did find the writing.

Josiah summoned the people to hear him read the book aloud. That inaugurated a reformation in the national life. Tragically, though, the king lost his life in a valiant but vain attempt to preserve the nation's independence by halting the advance of Egypt's armies to join forces with the Assyrian enemy. So the nation hastened on to its captivities a few years later. Even today one looks with sadness on the plain where that battle of Megiddo was fought and lost.

SELECTED READINGS

God has commanded advance to possess the land   1:6–8
The Ten Commandments are repeated   5:6–21
Moses' main address is largely a historical summary with a plea to remember God's good providences and be loyal to him.

Israel's creed   6:1–15
Verses 4–9 of this second chapter in Moses' second address have long been a Hebrew confession of faith—the Shema, named from the first word, meaning "hear." Verse 5, on love for God, has been called "the best-loved verse in the Old Testament."

A plea to remember God's goodness   8:1–17
The advice ascribed to Moses in verses 11–14 remains as pertinent as ever: *Take heed, lest . . . when you have eaten and are full . . . your heart be lifted up and you forget the Lord, your God. . . .* Words of verse 3 were quoted at Jesus' temptation (Luke 4:4).

Laws on clean and unclean foods   14:3–20
Frequent references to these matters appear in the New Testament and concern devout Jews today.

Choose life, not death   30:15–20
This teaching from Moses' third address, on loyalty, appears frequently in the whole Bible: to serve God and live lovingly is a matter of life or death.

Moses concludes his work   31:1–34:12

JOSHUA

After the death of Moses . . . (1:1a)

While the Jews were exiles in Babylon during the sixth century before Christ they could not bear to think that future generations might not have the story of their past. So, by about 550–500 B.C. Jewish patriots had completed the books we know as Joshua, Judges, Samuel, and Kings.

Joshua opens when the Israelites, on the march after the wilderness waiting, are encamped just east of the Jordan. The time may be not long after 1300 B.C. Moses had died but left behind a ready people, numbering some thousands, with Joshua, a former minister of his, as their new leader.

On a small scale the following era is like the beginnings of America's colonization. Canaan was occupied by native tribes who lived in walled "village-states," with warring "kings." They would resist the invaders and defend their territories to the death.

The initial objective for Israel's conquest was Jericho, almost in sight across the river. The town covered a few acres enclosed by walls whose deep foundations, thousands of years old, can be seen today. Men, women, children, and flocks made a precarious crossing of the Jordan. Then Jericho and town after town fell before them until all the Hebrew tribes were settled on the land.

The latter half of the Joshua book includes notes on the geographical distribution of the tribes. We most often say they were twelve but the tribe of Levi, designated to furnish priests for all, was not counted among the twelve. The tribes go by the names of Jacob's sons except that Joseph is represented by two with the names of his sons, Ephraim and Manasseh.

Chapters 23 and 24 contain the appealing farewell of the aging Joshua. It had been a bloody time and would continue to be. But he had kept alive the family that bore God's purpose to bless all nations and he could be buried in the ancient home of Abraham.

In that farewell to his people (24:14) Joshua pleaded: *fear the Lord and serve him in sincerity and faithfulness.* Exactly what fear of God with sincere and faithful service means when armed conflict is involved has never been easy to decide. Surely, though, no one will question the nobility of Joshua's ideal that seems a sky's distance from the warring practices of twentieth-century nations. Besides, now we have Christ's infinitely loftier appeal for love in action.

SELECTED READINGS

Joshua and Israel are to conquer and occupy Canaan   1:1–9
The journey begun in the Exodus will be completed. Confidence in God's favor will overbalance the Hebrews' lack of armament.

Jericho is besieged, captured, and utterly destroyed   6:1–2
Archaeologists believe this is the oldest living city.

A summary of Joshua's conquests; he allots the land   11:16–14:5
Joshua says farewell (in two accounts)   23:1–24:15
His people in the land of Promise, the old warrior's work is done.

God and Israel renew their covenant   24:16–28
He will work his purpose through these people though they could scarcely imagine its climax in Christ's coming so many centuries later.

JUDGES

After the death of Joshua . . . (1:1a)

Judges is a second book to report the Hebrews' conquest and settlement in Canaan. As in the era of America's Indian war, native tribes in Canaan tried to overrun the new colonies and drive the colonists out. Yet the book can tell how the newcomers held their ground and extended their frontiers through passing decades.

The Hebrew leaders, until about 1020 B.C. when central government under King Saul would develop, are known as judges. Thirteen of the fifteen are mentioned in this book, Eli and Samuel in First Samuel. These men, and one woman, not so much like our judges, were tribal heroes who appeared in critical times to lead their countrymen against Canaanite attacks.

In these times a persistent pattern of national behavior appears. Israel had the mission of serving God's purpose but was prone to failure. The historian has to repeat too often how a judge arose and delivered the Israelites but again they *did what was evil in the sight of the Lord* (2:11). As always, God has to teach his lessons repeatedly. Further, the judges themselves were not altogether saintly and, while we can learn from all of them, quite often it is what not to be or do.

One of the most interesting judges was Deborah, a Hebrew Joan of Arc. Her story is told in Chapter 4 and again in "Deborah's Song," a poem in 5:2–31. A Canaanite army, led by a Canaanite general Sisera, was threatening. Deborah called for 40,000 volunteers but only 10,000 rallied. The Canaanites even (4:3) *had nine hundred chariots of iron . . .* , but a violent rainstorm favored the Hebrews. *From heaven fought the stars,* says the poem (5:20).

Near the poem's end the mother of the enemy general, killed by Jael though his mother did not know it, listens for the sound of his chariot bringing him home. So we read that the mother (of Sisera) looked out a window and cried (5:28) *Why is his chariot so long in coming?* How much longer must mothers be losing sons in war?

SELECTED READINGS

God provides judges despite Hebrew unfaithfulness	2:11–23
"Deborah's Song"; a woman judge is victorious	5:2–31
Gideon turns back a Midianite invasion	6:1–7:25

Midianites were a camel-riding desert people from the East. Discipline, with a stratagem that resulted in fear and confusion, was more important than quantities of men and arms.

Jephthah keeps a hasty vow; sacrifices his daughter	11:29–40
Samson ends an eventful life	16:4–31

The entire story is in Chapters 13–16. Samson was expected to deliver the Israelite settlers from the Philistines who had entered the seacoast area about 1200 B.C. But the two groups would have to coexist for a long time. The New Testament has a story about a foolish rich man; the Old Testament has this one about a foolish strong man.

RUTH

> . . . your people shall be my people . . . your God my God
> . . . (1:16b)

Ruth has been called the "loveliest idyll in the language." A short story with a purpose, it is a sort of parable written against a background of history. Because the plot is laid in the judges' days the book appears after Judges. However, scholars say it was written to protest Ezra's campaign against mixed marriages of Jews and non-Jews, perhaps 450–400 B.C.

When famine struck Israel, Elimelech of Bethlehem emigrated with his wife Naomi and two sons across the Jordan into "foreign" Moab. There Mahlon and Chilion married native women, Ruth and Orpah. When, in ten years, all the women were left widowed, Naomi decided to return to Bethlehem.

After Ruth and Orpah had walked a short distance on the way with her she urged them to return to their people. But Ruth, putting compassion above home ties, declined with those noble words (1:16): *Entreat me not to leave you . . . for where you go, I will go, and where you lodge I will lodge; your people shall be my people, and your God my God. . . .*

Back in Bethlehem kindly Ruth began to support her mother-in-law as well as herself. It was time for harvesting barley and Ruth went into the fields of Boaz for the hard, hot work of gleaning. He directed his men to reap so that there would be more grain for the young widow to glean. In short, Boaz married Ruth and she bore him a son, Obed, father of Jesse, father of David. Thus Ruth, a Moabite, and not a Jewess, became David's great-grandmother.

Some great writer had seen that Israel was not meant to be a special garden of faith from which the peoples of other races were to be shut out forever.

The book remains to rebuke twentieth-century racists.

SELECTED READINGS

It will be best to read the whole book, possibly omitting 3:1–4:12 whose meaning requires knowledge of ancient customs.

FIRST SAMUEL and SECOND SAMUEL

Behold, to obey is better than sacrifice . . . (1 Sam. 15:22)

These two books, with the two books of Kings that follow, cover 500 years of Hebrew history. The historians, exiles in Babylonia, had likely completed all of them by 450 B.C.

The Samuel books alone cover the history of a century, about 1060 to 960 B.C. (We are able now to have reasonably accurate dating.) They have their name because the first seven chapters tell the story of that last of the judges, also called prophet and priest. The four books of Samuel and Kings would equal a modern history book of 200 pages, but our historians would confine themselves to facts while these emphasize lessons for godly living.

The authors could see that people and leaders had made serious mistakes. Israel had its divine mission: to serve God and the world, even with suffering rather than glory. To this God-given purpose it was only sometimes faithful. So the nation moved toward the pitiable disasters the historians had finally to record.

Meantime the truly great leaders this and following centuries produced were the prophets. There were "literary" ones from whom we have books later in the Bible; prominent, too, were "pre-literary" ones such as this Samuel, Nathan, Elijah, and Elisha.

First Samuel opens when Israel is about to have her first king and the once enslaved tribes will be a proud nation. Meantime a strong leader was needed. The book tells us first how Samuel's father Elkanah and his mother Hannah had dedicated him for God's service from his birth. True to that commitment through a long life he was perhaps Israel's greatest judge. Near the end of his career Samuel linked the periods of the judges and the monarchs. The people had pled with him to name a king. He warned them about the despotic and prodigal ways of kings and argued that God was king over Israel. The people would not be disuaded; Samuel anointed Saul (10:1, 2) to fill the post as Israel's first king.

First Samuel also tells those fascinating stories about the rise of David to be Israel's second king: About Jonathan, crown prince, and his brotherhood with David the shepherd boy. About David's struggles with jealous Saul who would have done away with him had not David taken refuge in the hills and caves of Judea. Finally, the book reports the death of Saul in battle with the Philistines where he perished with his three sons, Jonathan among them. Only David would break Philistine power forever.

Second Samuel opens with an elegy ascribed to the poetic David as he mourned over the deaths of Saul and Jonathan. Anointed king by the people of Judah, he reigned over them for seven and a half years, then he ruled the united monarchy for about forty years, 1010 to 971.

Among David's greater achievements was the capture of Jerusalem and its establishment as the political capital of an empire. By bringing the ark to Jerusalem he made it also the center of worship and planned for Solomon to build a temple there.

David also extended the boundaries of the nation to the farthest point in biblical history. But he added territory by subduing other peoples and contracting marriages with foreign princesses. This led to personal tragedies and palace intrigues painful to him and hurtful to the country.

An unhappy example of David's less noble traits is his sin with Bathsheba, wife of Uriah whom he sent to death in battle. The prophet Nathan condemned him with the memorable parable of the one ewe lamb owned by a poor man. He warned the king that the sword *shall never depart from your house.* So it was. There were battles with neighboring foes and David's son Absalom led a rebellion against his father that forced the king to flee Jerusalem. In the ensuing battle Absalom was killed in an accident and we hear David's plaintive cry, *O my son Absalom, my son, my son Absalom!* (18:33). The end of it all: later Israel will expect its Messiah to come from *the house of David.*

SELECTED READINGS

First Samuel

Samuel is "lent" to the Lord; brought up by priest Eli	1:9–28
Samuel is called as Israel's priest, prophet, last judge	3:2–4:1a
The people demand a king	8:4–22

Here is the ideal of Israel's greatest minds: let God rule.

Saul (reigning about 1020 to 1000) is Israel's first king	10:17–24
Samuel anoints David as second king	16:1–13

Saul is failing in mind and morale, so uncrowned David rises to prominence, arousing Saul's enmity.

David slays Philistines' Goliath; they remain enemies	17:1–58
David and Jonathan are devoted friends	18:1–11; 19:1–7; 20:1–42

Jonathan is "crown prince" but David is Saul's successor.

David, fugitive, spares Saul; the king relents briefly	26:1–25
Threatened by Philistines, Saul consults a medium at Endor, instead of seeking God's guidance	28:7–25
Defeated, Saul perishes along with Jonathan	31:1–13

Second Samuel

David laments the loss of Saul and Jonathan	1:17–27

The Song of the Bow is quoted from an earlier book of Jashar.

David reigns over Israel; makes Jerusalem capital	5:1–12

In conflict with Saul's heirs, he reigned first over Judah only.

David brings the ark into Jerusalem	6:12–15

Today Jerusalem is Holy City for Jews, Christians, Mohammedans.

David takes Bathsheba; Nathan speaks; Solomon is born	11:1–12:25

The Bible does not omit tainted spots in Hebrew history.

Absalom rebels against David and dies in an accident	18:9–33

Even kings suffer from failings and fates of their children.

David gets water to drink from the well at Bethlehem	23:13–17

David was a most beloved king though he weakened the kingdom.

David buys Araunah's threshing floor   **24:15–25**

The site of three temples is now covered by a Mohammedan shrine.

FIRST KINGS and SECOND KINGS

So Solomon sat upon the throne of David his father. . . .
(1 Kings 2:12)

Two books of Kings continue the history of the Hebrew monarchy from the end of David's reign to the Babylonian captivities, 961–587. The nation, in the vigor of early manhood, reaches its prime before Chapter 11. At the end it is all but dead, never to rise above fitful second childhood until present Israel came into being.

The first volume records especially the rise, glory, and decline of Solomon (961–922). A divided nation follows. A Northern Kingdom, capital at Samaria, includes ten tribes; two, Judah and Benjamin, comprise Judah, the Southern Kingdom centered at Jerusalem. The second volume of Kings tells how after two centuries the North is overrun by Assyria and its people taken captive to Assyria, never to return. Later by 125 years, Judah succumbs to the Babylonian Nebuchadnezzar who deports its people.

Altogether there were forty-two monarchs: three kings for United Israel, nineteen for each, North and South, plus a queen for Judah. The Books of Kings include the reigns of Solomon, third monarch of the union, and all those of the divided kingdom. Selected readings can sample only a few.

Fortunately, we are living in an era when archaeologists have uncovered evidence that certifies the facts of these and other biblical records. Remains of Solomon's copper industry can be seen. A wall built by Omri still stands on the hill of Samaria where he established the capital of Israel. There are many, many other instances.

First Kings, by its second chapter, tells how Solomon ascended the throne. This king's personal glory is perhaps the key to Israel's ultimate tragedy despite his mistaken reputation as the wisest of all men. He must, indeed, have had gifts of mind; doubtless he was shrewd, but rulers need character, too.

When David died, Solomon banished or killed any rivals for the throne, including Adonijah, heir apparent. Then he developed industry so that we read about great stables, mines, and ships. Yet he did not share the wealth with the people who produced it; instead they paid insufferable taxes and endured forced labor.

Solomon is perhaps remembered most favorably for the temple he built. Yet this was only one structure in the royal building program. There were lavish palaces for the king and his queens. These took thirteen years to build, while the temple was finished in seven. At the end Solomon had borrowed so heavily that he had to pay with twenty villages of Galilee. The follies of political power and prosperity can lead to national decay!

Rebellion broke over the head of Solomon's son Rehoboam who was even less wise and good than his father. He refused to reduce the burdens of his subjects and thereby split the kingdom. A former labor leader became Jeroboam I, king of the ten tribes of the Northern Kingdom. Then Rehoboam ruled over only Judah and Benjamin. The book closes with 11 chapters on lives, deeds, and evaluations of 13 of the 39 sovereigns of North and South. Of some it is said that they *did what was right in the eyes of the Lord* . . . ; others *did what was evil.* . . .

Second Kings reports the reigns of the remaining 26 rulers including their frequent wars with each other and other kingdoms. It is devoted chiefly to the end of it all. Israel, North, met its fate in 721. The last king was Hosea who, while paying tribute to Assyria, conspired with Egypt and had to pay the price for disloyalty. Assyrian Sargon II took Samaria and led away the ten tribes in everlasting captivity. Samaritans at the time of Christ, and some two hundred living still, are descendants of the few Hebrews who, left on the land, mixed with the refugees from other lands who replaced those taken away.

This record is most notable for its connection with the work of the first "literary prophet," Amos. Two or three decades before Samaria's fall he came from his shepherding beyond Bethlehem to plead with king and people to cease their folly and faithfully serve God. The luxury of the upper classes and their exploitation of the lower classes was scandalous. Samaria sent the prophet home and rolled on to its doom.

At the end of Second Kings we witness the death of Jerusalem. For its disloyalty, Nebuchadnezzar of Babylonia laid siege to the city and took away all but the dregs of the population. However, some captives or their children did return at the end of fifty years. A last chapter tells how Zedekiah, last in the line of Saul, David, and Solomon was carried away blinded after he had seen his sons slain.

SELECTED READINGS

First Kings

Solomon "establishes" his kingdom   **2:13–46**
Such savagery is known in later times, but never to be condoned.

Solomon dreams that he chose wisdom and demonstrates it   **3:3–28**
The demonstration may have been clever but scarcely commendable.

Solomon completes a temple in seven years, palaces in thirteen years   **6:1–10,37,38; 7:1–12**
Solomon dedicates the temple and pays for his buildings   **8:1–9:14**
The Queen of Sheba visits Solomon   **10:1–13**
Emperors of Ethiopia have considered themselves descendants.

Solomon grows rich and marries many wives   **10:14–11:8**
They introduced pagan religion that corrupted Hebrew faith.

The kingdom will be divided after Solomon's death   **11:9–13**
Rehoboam (922–915) becomes king of Judah, the South; Jeroboam I (922–901) of Israel, the North   **12:1–20**
Elijah battles for the Lord against Baal   **18:17–19:18**
Baal worship was a lewd and violent religion fostered by Jezebel, queen of Ahab. Child sacrifice was known in it. Elijah, known as greatest of "pre-literary prophets," kept sparks of faith alive.

Elisha, healer and revolutionary, is to succeed Elijah   19:19–21
Elijah scolds Ahab and Jezebel who seize Naboth's garden   21:1–29

Second Kings

Elijah departs; Elisha succeeds him   2:1–12a
Elisha heals Naaman, a Syrian leper   5:1–14
Sargon II captures Samaria; deports captives, 721 B.C.   17:1–6
Sennacherib of Assyria threatening Jerusalem, prophet Isaiah en-
courages King Hezekiah (715–687) to stand fast   19:14–37
His army smitten in some manner, Sennacherib withdraws.

Josiah (640–609), one of the nobler kings, repairs the temple; the
Deuteronomic Code is found and a reformation begins   22:1–23:3
The first Babylonian captivity occurs, 597   24:8–17
King Jehoiakim (609–598) had rebelled against Nebuchadnezzar.

Babylonian Nebuchadnezzar takes Jerusalem (587)   24:18–25:12
Zedekiah (597–587) too, rebelled; exile will last half century.

FIRST CHRONICLES and SECOND CHRONICLES; EZRA and NEHEMIAH
Adam . . . Solomon . . . David . . . Cyrus

Affairs of the Hebrew nation have already been traced from
its rise through its fall. First and Second Chronicles cover the
same ground but begin with Adam and continue until the exile
is about to end. The Chronicles books are usually associated with
the ones called Ezra and Nehemiah. The four not only tell again
the stories in Samuel and Kings, they also follow Israel's history
through a century and a half after the exile. They do this with
an extraordinary emphasis on religion, paying more attention to
a king's zeal for Judaism than for his personal righteousness and
public service.

Who was the author of the four books? He is called The
Chronicler whose work in one part bears the name of Ezra and
includes what seem to be memoirs of Nehemiah. The Chronicler

was a Jerusalem "Jew of Jews." For him Judah had been a nation above all others, especially her sister Israel. His attention centers on Judah's heroes, David and Solomon, with blindness toward their weaknesses. He is devoted to the law and especially interested in corporate worship. Perhaps he was himself a Levite.

When were the books completed? The favored answer is around 400 B.C. Jerusalem then was only a little colony of Jews living in political subjection to Persia and in poverty. Religious revival was needed. The four books were likely meant to correct discouragement and apathy in the colony.

First Chronicles, Chapter 1, traces Hebrew genealogies beginning with Abraham and ending with Jacob. Chapters 2 through 9 deal with the *sons of Israel*, one by one. Chapter 10, almost word for word, repeats the Samuel-Kings account of Saul's death. David's reign occupies Chapters 11 through 29. Chapter 11 repeats from Second Samuel 5 the choosing of David to be King. This Levite sees David supremely as the one who brought the ark to Jerusalem and prepared for building "Solomon's temple."

Second Chronicles, in its first nine chapters, deals with the reign of Solomon. Chapter 1 includes his famous request for God to give him wisdom. Doubtless it seems harsh to say that he knew what he needed. As The Chronicler tells it, God promised him also *riches, possessions*, and *honor*. According to one verse, God *made silver and gold as common in Jerusalem as stone . . .* (1:15). But the author says nothing about the disastrous cost and tragic results of the king's storied glory.

There follows, 10:1–36:21, the history of Southern Judah—not also of the North—from the reign of Rehoboam (922–915), first king, through the final catastrophe under the last king, Zedekiah (597–587). The chapters mention Judah's monarchs in order, rating them good or bad according to their religious attitudes and achievements. A last chapter concludes (36:22, 23) with the proclamation of Cyrus, 536 B.C., permitting exiles who chose that course to return home and build a new temple.

Ezra and *Nehemiah*, the books, cover the return and chief events in the century following: (a) arrival of the first returning exiles, 536; (b) completion of Zerubbabel's temple, 516 (a story

told also by Haggai and Zechariah); (c) arrival and work of
Ezra and Nehemiah, somewhere between 450 and 400.

Former captives had been treated better than we may have
supposed. They were settled in little colonies where they could
lead reasonably normal lives as farmers or businessmen and
have such religious leaders as the prophet Ezekiel. Their priests
could be busy completing what are now the biblical books we
are studying. Yet, some Jews, even after fifty years, yearned for
a return to Jerusalem. Cyrus the Persian provided the oppor-
tunity. An enlightened monarch who allowed deported popula-
tions in his realm to return home, he issued a decree permitting
a contingent of Hebrews to go to Jerusalem. The first group arrived with families, servants, and equipment in 536. In a way it
can be said that their caravan was bringing the world its Bible
and Christianity.

Ezra, the man, did not arrive until many decades later. Then
another Persian king, Artaxerxes I, gave him authority over religious matters in Jerusalem. It was he who, it is thought, brought
with him the Pentateuch with its Priestly Code, that rendering
of the law which we read in Lev. 17–26, 28. Then, one morning,
the people gathered in the public square to hear him reading the
book of the law (Neh. 8:1–12).

It may be said that Ezra accomplished reforms that helped
preserve the Jewish people through whom Jesus was born. However, the book closes with his cruel effort to dissolve mixed
marriage between Jewish men and people on the land, even of
those who had brought Babylonian wives. His purpose was to
keep Hebrew blood pure and the nation unified. Yet it is not a
pretty picture where the "guilty" are assembled in *heavy rain* for
non-Jewish wives and half-breed children to be separated from
Jewish husbands and fathers. So Ezra stands as a warning against
zealotry that lacks human understanding and a loving spirit.

When Nehemiah came he busied himself with practical needs
of the municipality. Nearly a century and a half after Jerusalem's
walls had been breached, they were not repaired—nearly three
miles of them with ten gates and five towers of defense. Meantime the city was encircled by spiteful enemies who harassed

these intruders into the territory the former had seized. Nehemiah had been cupbearer to king Artaxerxes from whom he had a commission as governor of Jerusalem with instructions to rebuild those walls. He began with what we would call a survey. Before he finished he had to beat back numerous attempts to halt the work—one time as if the workmen labored with a trowel in one hand and a sword in the other. Yet the work was completed in record time and an appropriate service of celebration was held.

When now we read in the fifty-first psalm *rebuild the walls of Jerusalem . . .* it can challenge persons to undertake the work of the churches with Nehemiah's spirit.

SELECTED READINGS

First Chronicles

Genealogies begin with Adam   1:1–4

They continue through nine chapters. Here is new material.

Saul perishes and David becomes Israel's second king   10:1–11:9

To see how The Chronicler retells older narratives, the passage can be compared with 1 Sam. 31 and 2 Sam. 5:1–12.

David prepares for building the temple   28:1–29:10

Second Chronicles

Solomon asks for wisdom, gets great possessions   1:7–17
The king will build his temple   2:1–18
Cyrus proclaims return to Jerusalem and the building of a new temple
there   36:22,23

Ezra

A group of exiles prepares to return   1:1–7
The people lay foundations for the new temple   3:8–13

See Haggai and Zechariah for details of the building.

The second temple, Zerubbabel's, is dedicated   6:13–22

The third, last temple, Herod's, was being built at Christ's time.

| Ezra arrives in Jerusalem; he teaches the law | 7:1–10 |
| Ezra separates Hebrew men from alien wives and children | 10:1–17 |

There is another account in Neh. 8:1–12.

Nehemiah

| Nehemiah comes to Jerusalem with a royal commission | 1:11b–2:8 |
| Nehemiah will repair the city's broken walls | 2:11–20 |

After three days he begins with an inspection at night.

The Jews repel neighboring enemies as they work	4:15–23
The wall is finished in 52 days	6:15,16
The people hear the law and pledge allegiance to it	8:1–12

ESTHER

And who knows whether you have not come to the king-dom for such a time as this? (4:14)

Some would say this book is a type of historical novel. It is certainly a fascinating and dramatic story with a beautiful heroine, a patriotic hero, and a scandalous villain. It has a happy ending, too. Although, strangely, the book does not mention the name of God, there is ample reason for a place in the Bible. It probably comes from some date between 350 and 250 B.C., long after the event it commemorates but when its lessons may have been gravely needed as they have long been.

According to the plot, when the Jews in Persia were once threatened with massacre a heroic young woman saved her people from disaster, and they even visited the threat upon their oppressors. Tradition has it that the first Feast of Purim celebrated this event. Now, each March, Jews celebrate the feast again and read Esther to explain its origin. Jews everywhere then can give thanks for their own deliverances and feel assured that God will preserve them despite persecution.

The book breathes a spirit of racial conflict in deep contrast with the universal brotherhood taught in the books of Ruth and Jonah. Yet it should be a powerful antidote against anti-Semitism.

In a century when six million Jews and more were slaughtered in Europe the world still needs to learn that they, too, are children of the one Father of all. No less we can always honor the sacrificial devotion of an Esther. Too, the book has reinforced through the centuries a needed trust in God's steadfast love for others as well as Jews.

SELECTED READINGS
It will be best to read the entire book, remembering throughout that Esther was a Jewess.

Books of Wisdom and Poetry

Even a casual reader of the Old Testament knows it contains many kinds of writing. The Hebrews had not only historians, lawyers, and priests; they had also "sages" or "wisemen," and poets.

Although works of sages appear in many passages, these men left us three biblical books: Job, Proverbs, and Ecclesiastes. Typical wisdom literature, in substance, does not refer to learning of philosophers or scientists. Usually it is the shrewd thinking of persons who have arrived through life's experiences at what they consider lively common sense. Sages were earnest seekers after the good life who aimed to teach others, especially youth, how to avoid life's dangerous pitfalls and enjoy its brightest promises. With the best of them, good life is to be dominated by a religious spirit; as they put it in Prov. 9:10, *The fear of the Lord is the beginning of wisdom.* Yet some of their wisdom can be called "prudential ethics" that needs to be tested by Christian standards.

Job, quite different, is a great work of literary art. In the form of a dramatic poem it upholds a lofty view of God while dealing with the troublous problem of human suffering. Proverbs is, more simply, a series of short and pithy statements about successful living. Ecclesiastes is a sort of debate about life's meaning. These three books speak to Everyman on three perplexities:

What shall I think and do in the hour of trial?
How can I live my life most effectively and happily?
What is a proper and God-given purpose for my life?

The Hebrews had their poets, too. We see it more readily now in The Revised Standard Version where poetry is printed in poetic form. It appears through the Old Testament from Gen. 2 to Zech. 13 and there is also New Testament poetry.

Most English poems have four elements of beauty: vivid imagery, lofty thought, orderly rhythm, and rhyme. Hebrew poetry is more like free verse, lacking regular meter and rhyme. But it has parallelism or sense rhythm, a balancing of line against line according to meaning. Here is a simple example (Ps. 19:1):

> *The heavens are telling the glory of God;*
> *and the firmament proclaims his handiwork.*

Old Testament poets left us three complete books: Psalms, Song of Solomon, and Lamentations. Actually, though, nearly a third of the Old Testament is poetry, much of it in the prophets. Almost every possible type is represented: drama, elegy, folksong, nature ode, patriotic hymn, personal petition, and praise.

Biblical poetry can serve us in three ways. It can stir our minds to think a poet's thoughts after him. It can call up our profounder sentiments so that we feel as the poet felt. Most of all, it can fashion our patterns of action. Altogether poetry can "whisper the music" out of a human being.

JOB

I had heard of thee by the hearing of the ear; but now my eye sees thee . . . (42:5)

Why do good people suffer? Is Satan at work tempting and testing them? Is God unjust or does he punish in proportion to sin? Has the seemingly good person sinned secretly? Does God send suffering as chastisement to correct wrongdoing and elicit righteousness? Do we suffer for the sake of others? Does suffering redeem? Job's author struggles with these questions but scarcely provides final answers. We may only conclude that the questions point to half-truths. Yet there is more in Job.

The book is well described as an "autobiography of a soul battling against despair." He was prosperous, happy, blessed in his family and his religion. Then disaster strikes; he loses everything including his health. In deep distress and soul-searching he cries out repeatedly, "Why?" In the end he does not have the kind of answer he was seeking or we would like him to have had. He does arrive at another kind of solution to his problem. He moves from turmoil of spirit to peace for his soul. If the final teaching of the book can be put briefly: God is great, righteous, and good; trust his loving care in adversity as well as in prosperity.

Job, they say, was first a folk story, possibly as old as 1000 B.C. An author, perhaps in the 300s B.C., split it into two parts and put his poems between them like making a sandwich. The high point in the book is reached when the author lets God speak in those breath-taking concepts of Chapters 38 through 42 and Job's replies. Anyone who has not read these chapters has missed the grandest biblical literature outside the New Testament.

SELECTED READINGS

Job, under Satan's testing, meets misfortune   1:1–2:13

The Old Testament sometimes seems to teach: be bad and suffer; be good and prosper. Thinking that such simple notions of penalty and reward are inadequate and really Satan's doctrine, this author lets God disprove them. No one can say Job was good just because it pays.

Three friends debate Job's problem with him   4:1–30:31

While Job sits among the ashes of his life, lamenting the day of his birth, three friends visit the stricken man. As each speaks three times, Job replies.

Job is innocent of sin that merits terrible suffering   31:1–40

He concludes this argument with his "oath of clearing" that denies a frequent explanation for suffering.

Elihu speaks four times with Job replying   32:1–37:24

The younger man is angry because Job *justified himself rather than God* and because *there was no answer in the mouths . . .* of the three elders. Perhaps, he argues, affliction will be the means of Job's purification (36:22): *Who is a teacher like* [God]?

The author lets God speak three times, Job twice   38:1–39:30

God's first address brings Job face to face with the Immeasurable Greatness seen in the things of nature.

Job, overwhelmed, replies to the Lord in submission, penitence, retraction, and trust   40:3–5; 42:1–6

Epilog: Job's former life is restored and enhanced   42:7–17

Job has learned, as Paul did (Phil. 4:12): *how to be abased* as well as *how to abound* willingly in the hands of God.

PSALMS

Let everything that breathes praise the Lord! (150:6a)

This book is a collection of the best-loved religious poems of the greatest Hebrew poets who wrote through a thousand years of history. The collection was assembled gradually until our book was completed perhaps as recently as 200 years before Christ.

Psalmists were deeply religious souls sometimes shouting, sometimes grieving, sometimes soothing. Always they mirrored mankind's rebellions and loyalties, strivings and struggles, agonies and triumphs at their most intensely real. Amazingly, familiarity with the poems will disclose that there is scarcely an attribute of God not celebrated in them; also there is scarcely a human concern for which there is no helpful message.

The date of any particular psalm and its author's name are usually uncertain. The mention of definite events and the nature of the language show that they were written by many persons in many eras. All were one time ascribed to David's authorship. Now we recognize that the biblical expression *a psalm of David* can mean a psalm to, for, connected with, or something else about David. It need not mean he was the author.

From its earliest beginnings Psalms must have been a devotional handbook and hymnbook. Jesus quoted the psalms; apostles remembered them in their epistles. They belonged to later saints and martyrs, crusaders and reformers, missionaries of ancient and modern days carrying the cross to unbelievers on every continent—all these, along with humble pastors and lay persons of every century. Now Psalms is an interfaith manual with all bodies of Christians joining Jews in psalmic reading, group recital, liturgy, solo, chorus, and hymn. Every minute of every day, somewhere in every clime, Christians and Jews alike are echoing the sentiments that for three thousand years have expressed the deepest religious experiences of uncounted billions of God's people. There is no other book like this!

SELECTED READINGS

" . . . the Lord knows the way of the righteous . . ."   1:1–6
Who is the righteous person? Who is the wicked one? What happens to each?

"O Lord, heal me . . . "   6:1–7
The poet pleads for deliverance from sickness and death by the God of steadfast love. He moans and weeps but his tone changes as he says *the Lord accepts my prayer.*

"When I look at thy heavens . . . "   8:1–9
Stirred by the beauty of starry night, a poet praises the Creator who made the earth and gave man dominion over it. We like to use his poem as we think of the great and lovely out-of-doors.

" . . . he is at my right hand . . . "   16:1–11
Like James (1:17) this poet is saying *every perfect gift is from above.* . . . He mentions a dozen gifts from the Source and his whole being responds to the blessings of security and joy.

"Let the words of my mouth . . . be acceptable . . . "   19:1–14
A modern man said that two things fill the mind with admira-

tion: "the starry heavens above and the moral law within." This psalmist praises the God whom nature and the law reveal.

"I shall not want . . . "   23:1–6
In this best loved psalm of all, God is gracious host at table as well as tender shepherd. Trust in God's lovingkindness is a frequent theme throughout the psalm.

" . . . thou didst forgive the guilt of my sin . . . "   32:1–11
As if in a beatitude, the psalmist is declaring: Oh, the happiness of a forgiven sinner! His soul was in distress when he *declared not [his] sin*. Now he calls on all righteous to *shout for joy*.

"Why are you cast down, O my soul . . . ? Hope in God . . . "
42:1–11
Of all the types of psalms, those of personal supplication appear most often. This "plaintive prayer of a man in time of crisis" is one of the choicest. His enemies taunt him, *Where is your God?* He can reply *I shall again praise him, my help and my God.*

"Create in me a clean heart, O God . . . "   51:1–19
Seven psalms are called "penitential"; this is the best known. Its poet's cry for pardon, cleansing, and renewal speaks so well the pleas of persons in private or public confession.

"Thou visitest the earth and waterest it . . ."   65:1–13
A song for Thanksgiving day shows that the Hebrews were a grateful people though it often seems that they had little cause to be. To all it says, "Count your many blessings."

"In the day of my trouble I call on thee . . ."   86:1–17
A needy servant of God utters a cry of supplication. Not only begging relief, he adds, *Teach me thy way*. Then he gives thanks for God's steadfast love. A rather complete prayer.

" . . . thou has been our dwelling place in all generations." 90:1–17
Is this brief and troubled life worthwhile? Yes, there is an eternal home in God. It gives us our great modern hymn, "Our God, our help in ages past . . . and our eternal home."

"As a father pities his children, so the Lord . . . "   103:1–22

According to this "thanksgiving song of a forgiven man," God, in the Old Testament too, is the Father by whose steadfast love his people are redeemed.

" . . . he has heard my voice . . . "   116:1–19

A psalmist has been healed of an illness which brought him close to death. Perhaps recited first in the temple service when he brought his thank-offering, it is used still to thank God for recovery from illness.

"I have laid up thy word in my heart . . . "   119:11–16

Psalm 119, with 176 verses, is the longest of all. It is divided into 22 sections, one for each letter of the Hebrew alphabet. Also, each of the eight verses in each section begins with the same letter, for instance, Beth, our B. The theme is the same throughout: the law is a light and an aid.

"From whence does my help come?"   121:1–8

Psalms 120 through 134 are called Songs of Ascent, hymns for pilgrims on their way to Mt. Zion. They gaze on the hills ahead where, sooner or later, they will see, over the peaks, the temple of the God who has been their helper on the journey.

"Out of the depths I cry to thee, O Lord!"   130:1–8

The psalmist is in a "dark night of the soul." Like a man drowning, overwhelmed by guilt, he waits for God's words of forgiveness. Yet he can exclaim *hope in the Lord.*

"Let everything that breathes praise the Lord!"   150:1–6

Each of the five books in the collection closes with a doxology. Book V and the whole book end with this supreme one. It is a universal symphony in which, with full orchestra, all mankind and even animal life praise God.

PROVERBS

Wisdom cries aloud in the street . . . (1:20)

Proverbs is a characteristic piece of the wisdom literature prepared by those sages or wise men of Israel. Really a collection of eight collections of their work, this final edition is thought to have been completed in the third century before Christ. Although Solomon's name has been associated with the authorship of the entire book, only certain portions are directly ascribed to him. Perhaps the king was a patron of wise men who honored him by publishing the work in his name. Yet the sayings surely have come, like our proverbs, out of many persons' experiences.

Typical proverbs are short, pithy declarations, often poetic. Memorable maxims of conduct, they deal with almost every topic of ethical importance: business dealings and family relations, vice and virtue, poverty and riches, victory and defeat, mirth and sorrow. The sayings are sometimes sharp, even tinged with sarcasm or humor. The instructions can be viewed as sensible guides for living though the moral is sometimes on a practical rather than religious plane, scarcely representing Christian ideals.

Usually, as one writer has said, the proverbs put long experiences in short sentences. Sometimes, though, a wisdom writer produced a long passage like the poem with which the book ends.

SELECTED READINGS

Introducing the "proverbs of Solomon" and their use, the book presents short maxims on obedience to God and parents.

"Wisdom cries aloud in the street . . ."   1:20–33
As a woman, wisdom calls on persons to heed her. When they even laugh at her, she talks to herself about their coming calamity.

The worth of seeking and receiving wisdom   2:1–22
"Trust in the Lord with all your heart . . . "   3:5–12
Verses 11 and 12 on the Lord's discipline have been called "the most profound note in the book."

"Go to the ant . . . consider her ways."   6:6–19
This well-known passage names *six things the Lord hates.*

This proverb is reflected by Saint Paul in Romans 12:20.

A truly wise sage describes a *good wife* as efficient housekeeper,
devoted spouse and mother, and *woman who fears the Lord.*

ECCLESIASTES

Remember also your Creator in the days of your youth . . .
(12:1)

Many persons have said that Solomon wrote Ecclesiastes, too.
Actually we do not know who the original author was; besides,
his writing has been edited. Possibly the work was completed,
like the Proverbs, in the third century B.C.

The original author calls himself *The Preacher* but he is certainly different than our preachers. This world-weary soul found
that nothing is worthwhile. For him everything in nature or human society is vain, empty of value—learning, pleasure, wealth,
wisdom, and everything else. As he says, *All streams run to the*
sea but the sea is not full . . . (1:7). The poor fellow seems not
to have found a God to thank or a child of God to help and love.

Ecclesiastes has been called "the strangest book in the Old
Testament." Various solutions to the puzzle it presents have been
proposed. Some have said that wiser and more spiritually mature
men inserted rebuttals at various places in the old text. It is as if
three voices are speaking:

The Preacher: *. . . vanity of vanities. All is vanity.* (1:2)
A Sage: *Cast your bread upon the waters, for you will find*
it after many days. (11:1)
A Scribe: *Fear God and keep his commandments; for this is*
the whole duty of man. (12:13)

When studied carefully Ecclesiastes will answer one who asks,
"What's the use?" by saying, "Serve God and man."

SELECTED READINGS

The Preacher finds nothing worthwhile	1:1–11

The hopeless view of life: "You can't win."

Pleasure is futile and possessions are never sufficient	2:1–17
" . . . There is a season and a time . . . "	3:1–9
"A good name is better . . . "	7:1-13
"Remember also your Creator in the days of your youth . . ."	12:1–7

It is thought that The Preacher is portraying old age. Verse 7 is the most widely quoted passage of the book.

SONG OF SOLOMON

. . . for love is strong as death . . .(8:6)

Authorship of this book also has been attributed to Solomon because his name appears in the first verse. Present day scholars think it was possibly completed near the year 300 B.C., in the Greek period of Hebrew history.

Does it express an individual's love of God? Is it an allegory of God's love for the church? Or is it a collection of love lyrics or wedding songs as now most often said?

Realizing that God, having chosen to rear his children in families, does not despise the ties that bind man and woman in a fellowship of love we can understand why the book is in the Bible.

For these careless days, the Song has a strong message about constancy in love that is real (8:6, 7): *Set me as a seal upon your heart . . . for love is strong as death. . . . If a man offered for love all the wealth of his house, it would be utterly scorned.*

A book that may seem to be on the fringes of the Bible discloses the fullness of the biblical view of life.

SELECTED READINGS

It will be best to taste this book at one point or another, including perhaps Chapter 2 and the concluding 8:6, 7.

Lamentations, the third book of poetry,
comes after Jeremiah because it was
once thought to be that prophet's work.

Books of Prophetic Teaching

For those who know them well, the prophetic books are the treasure house in the Old Testament. Is there a concern of person or community for which these have no word with relevance and power? Yet no other biblical books are so sadly neglected and abused. This is due largely to tragic misunderstanding about the nature and work of Old Testament prophets. They were forthtellers, not primarily foretellers like weather prophets. They could foresee, in the light of history and current events, and did declare the evil threatening their people if they did not change their ways; they also had noble visions of what God would do in his mercy. Even so, predicting was not the essence of a prophet's work.

A prophet was one called to speak for another: God. He was a human spring bubbling forth from a hidden source: God. He was a seer able to understand what others could not about the relations of God and man. It is best to think of the prophets as teachers, preachers, and actors for God, communicating their word in various ways for the people of their time and, as it has happened, for all time.

The books may puzzle readers by their literary form and historical references. Regarding literary matters, much of the literature is poetry and must be understood like all other poetry. As one historical problem, while each piece of writing arose at a particular time in history, the Bible does not present the books in historical order. If arranged according to their dating they would likely appear in this more understandable order:

Amos	Habakkuk	Zechariah (1–8)
Hosea	Jeremiah	Malachi
Micah	Ezekiel	Joel
Isaiah (1–39)	Obadiah	Jonah
Zephaniah	Isaiah (40–66)	Zechariah (9–14)
Nahum	Haggai	Daniel

A few generalities of prophetic teaching must not be missed. Prophets taught that true prosperity and peace can be had only through living by the divine will. For a nation, clever political moves may even prove evil if they lead it away from devotion to God. Vastly important, no ritual ceremonies can take the place of personal trust in God with corresponding conduct.

Prophets dared to look toward a distant "happy ending" for the nation. God would forgive if its people were penitent. As for persons, *turn*, the prophets say, and *live*.

Prophets had a sensitive social consciousness. They saw a necessary connection between the way we love God and the way we love fellowmen. Our religion is void unless we are treating our neighbor with justice and mercy. We are not forgiven by God unless we are ready to forgive an offending neighbor.

The prophets mightily opposed the common preoccupation with material prosperity, especially when it was accompanied by indifference to human rights, needs, and dignity.

The proper way to discover such presently useful teaching values in prophetic books is to ask:

What was this prophet enabled to see or hear from God?

What was he teaching about people's problems in his day?

What is he saying to us, me, now?

ISAIAH

If you will not believe, surely you shall not be established. (7:9b)

This first of the sixteen books by prophets is best known for a passage we hear each Christmas season (9:6): *For unto us a child is born . . . his name will be called Wonderful Counselor, Mighty God, Everlasting Father, Prince of Peace.*

Although the book belongs among the greatest works of all literature it is not easy to understand. It came out of a tumultuous period in history; its principal ideas are profound. In addition, the book probably includes the work of three or more writers. Chapters 1 through 39 are called First Isaiah; chapters

40 through 55, second Isaiah. Certain scholars also say there is a Third Isaiah, Chapters 56–66, and there are editorial comments.

The prophet of First Isaiah was a nobleman, married, and the father of two sons. His ministry began about 740 B.C. and lasted until 701 B.C. Fostering the proper place of religion in politics, he served among the counselors of three of Judah's kings.

Chapter 6 tells the story of the prophet's call to speak for God. A serious-minded youth, he must have been troubled by the concern that perplexes so many: What shall I do with my life? It appears that he had thought about being a prophet but was afraid he was not good enough. One day in the temple, doubtless with his inner eye, he has a stirring vision. Overpowered by a sense of God's holiness and his lack of it, he sees that God needs him and will purify his life. This dialogue follows (6:8, 9):

The Lord: *Whom shall I send, and who will go for us?*
The prophet: *Here am I. Send me.*
The Lord: *Go and say to this people . . .*

Isaiah went and said until, likely, his ministry ended in martyrdom. Assyrian armies were driving westward and threatening Egypt. Little Judah was caught between the opposing powers, each trying to use her as a buffer state. Hoping to play safe she would ally herself with first one and then the other while Isaiah steadfastly taught: "God is holy; be a holy people; trust only Him."

In Isaiah we meet a theme that will be continued in the New Testament: the coming of a Messiah and a Messianic Age. "Messiah" means often "King," and "Messianic Age" the period of his reign. The prophets saw humanity's need for a more gracious king ruling over a fairer world. They believed that God wishes to provide such a destiny for humanity. Christ came and there have been those who realized that the Messiah has appeared. Perhaps the Hebrew hope can kindle a modern zeal to further that Messiah's gracious rule for us and through us.

With Chapter 40 at the beginning of Second Isaiah, the times, scenes, and persons of the book change. It is near the end of the exile. Faithful Jews in Babylon foresee a change of government that will permit their joyous return to Jerusalem. Cyrus, a Persian conqueror, will overthrow Babylon. Then, as is his habit, he will let displaced persons in his kingdom go home.

The great prophet of this happy time has been called "the poet of the one loving God for all the nations." His four Servant Songs make some scholars speak of him as the greatest mind in the Old Testament. The Servant, like the Messiah, is to usher in the nobler age with Israel as the agent to accomplish this. Christians would say that now the church stands in the place of responsibility and privilege that once belonged to Israel alone.

The Fourth Servant Song including (53:3) *He was . . . a man of sorrows, and acquainted with grief,* is the most frequently used passage of Second Isaiah. The great prophet sees, for us, that the world can be brought to God and godliness only if someone will care enough to suffer as Christ did. There remains, though, the dreadful need that his people suffer with him to complete the task his deed made possible.

If Third Isaiah came from a particular person he may have worked after the return to Jerusalem when, among the discouraged people, morals and religion were at a low ebb. It is out of such a time that we would have Chapters 56–66.

SELECTED READINGS
"First Isaiah"

The times of the prophet, 740–701 in Jerusalem   1:1–9
At once the prophet must lament: *Ah, sinful nation. . . .*

". . . cease to do evil; learn to do good."   1:10–20
Obedience, not celebrations, can make scarlet sins white as wool.

Jerusalem as she might be; nations without war   2:1–4
Isaiah sees God as judge over a peaceful world and Jerusalem as teacher of nations. Verse 4 is also in Mic. 4:3. The prophets were likely friends.

Jerusalem as she is: a vineyard yielding wild grapes   5:1–25
Isaiah is called and commissioned to be God's prophet   6:1–13

The priceless teaching of vicarious suffering for redemption.

Christ used these words to describe his mission (Luke 4:16-30).

A fitting conclusion for this most frequently used book of the prophets. It appears again in the Revelation to John.

JEREMIAH

The harvest is past, the summer is ended, and we are not saved. (8:20)

Jeremiah is an unusual book in five ways. First, it reports the manner of its writing. The story begins in 36:1-3 . . . *this word came to Jeremiah from the Lord: Take a scroll and write on it . . . so that every one may turn from his evil way, and that I may forgive. . . .* Jeremiah wrote by dictation to his scribe, Baruch. But King Jehoiakim burned the scroll. Then (36:27,28), Jeremiah was told: *Take another scroll and write on it all the former words.* Jeremiah wrote again, for God, in behalf of the penitent and forgiven life for everyone.

Second, Jeremiah was a man so extraordinary that he has been called "the prophet." His ministry lasted for a long generation beginning about 626 B.C. Then (1:6) *the Lord said to me . . . to whom I send you, you shall go, and whatever I command you you shall speak.* Jeremiah did go in spite of reluctance because of his youth and spoke though he was usually in peril as he strove to have his wavering nation find its security in faithfulness to God. It would seem that he could have spared himself by merely keeping silent. But he says (20:9) *there is in my heart as it were a burning fire shut up in my bones, and I am weary with holding it in. . . . I cannot.*

Third, this prophet ministered in the worst of times. The East and West of those days were wrestling for domination of their world. Judah became a satellite of Babylonia but her kings kept trusting Egypt to set her free. Twice the Babylonian overlords appeared at Jerusalem's gates to punish her for her disloyalty. In the end Nebuchadnezzar destroyed her and the anguished Jeremiah was there to watch the bitter end. Meantime, though he was considered a traitor, he could only advise the king to submit. Trust and serve God, he taught, he will restore an obedient and repentant people.

Fourth, this prophet left a new and particularly important message in his teaching of religion as a personal relation between an individual and his God. Rightly, each individual has, within himself, the responsibility to know and serve God.

Finally, Jeremiah's book reveals the why and how of the Bible's origin. The prophet had an inescapable mission from God; a God-kindled fire was raging within his spirit. What he wrote was as if he had taken a handful of the flaming fuel and placed it within the covers of the Book where it still glows ready to light other blazes.

SELECTED READINGS

Jeremiah's call and inaugural vision   1:1–19

The Hebrew word for "almond rod" being almost the same as for "watch over," the almond branch is a symbol of God's watching over his word to bring it to fruition. The boiling pot, blown by a North wind, is a threat of invasion by Scythians from the North.

Jeremiah's temple sermon; trust in the temple is vain   7:1–15
Jeremiah urges trust in God alone with repentance and obedience.

"Hear the words of this covenant ... "   11:1–8
Jeremiah was helping the good king Josiah to reform the nation. This passage may refer to Deuteronomy.

God and the house of Israel are like a potter and clay   18:1–11
Now we have the hymn, "Thou art the potter; I am the clay."

Jeremiah curses the day of his birth   20:1–18
Prophets were people! They could despair as well as rejoice.

Jeremiah writes exiles of the first captivity in Babylon   29:1–14
People are to be good and godly citizens wherever they are.

There is hope; the Lord will save   30:1–11
"The Book of Consolation" promises a restoration, as there was.

Jeremiah teaches inward and individual responsibility   31:27–34
Jeremiah is rescued from a cistern by an Ethiopian   38:1–13
The siege is on. Jeremiah teaches that it is useless to resist. The *princes* hope to silence him but fail.

The capture of the city and the "second captivity"   39:1–10
Jeremiah will serve those left on the land.   40:1–12

LAMENTATIONS

How lonely sits the city that was full of people! (1:1a)

Lamentations is a collection of dirges, sung amid suffering and sorrow after Jerusalem had fallen. Although a poetry book, it appears here because it was formerly viewed as the work of Jeremiah. It probably includes the work of several poets.

The first poet strikes the keynote (1:12): *Look and see if there is any sorrow like my sorrow.* Yet there is more in the five poems than a series of heartbroken cries. With a truer perspective than in the days when they had not counted their God-given blessings the poets now see Jerusalem's *precious things* for what they were. There had come a time when one could say (1:8) *The Lord is in the right for I have rebelled against his word.*

Through suffering, too, compassion for others was born in the place of blithe carelessness. Not enough persons in our own day have the sensitivity of the poet who wrote (2:11,12), *My heart is poured out in grief because . . . babes . . . cry to their mothers, where is bread . . . ?*

SELECTED READINGS

Perhaps Chapter 3 best expresses both the grief and the hope of the population remaining after the siege and captivity.

EZEKIEL

Son of man, stand upon your feet, and I will speak with you. (2:1)

Reading and study of the book of Ezekiel should begin with a brief review of Hebrew history. About 1300 years before Christ, Moses led a band of Hebrew slaves out of Egypt toward Palestine. Three hundred years later their descendants had conquered and settled that land and established a remarkable little kingdom under Saul, David, and Solomon. After an additional 400 years the same peoples had been plundered, their capital cities destroyed, and families driven into exile. Religious leaders went with the other captives, Ezekiel among them, taken in the "first captivity" when probably in his twenties.

The prophet's work began with a call and commission (1:28b–2:7) following an inaugural vision (1:1–28a). We have almost the exact date and place: June or July 592, along the Grand

Canal east of Babylon. There Ezekiel could live in a house of his own where others of the Jewish community-in-exile could hear him teach.

Ezekiel's account of his inaugural vision is an effort to describe the indescribable. As he writes of creatures, faces, wheels, wings, and eyes, certain interpreters say he is declaring the omniscience, omnipotence, sovereignty, and majesty of God as the ruler of the world.

Ezekiel's following ministry occurred in two periods, the final fall of Jerusalem marking the midpoint of his work and of the book. Twenty-four chapters deal with the period when he was looking on from afar as Jerusalem hurried to her doom. Another twenty-four report his effort to keep hope alive among the homesick and disheartened exiles. Among other things he prepared "Ezekiel's Code" (40–48), laws to use when they would, as he told them they surely would, return to Jerusalem.

In Ezekiel's teaching he was fond of role-acting his message. He built toy figures to mimic a siege of Jerusalem. Lying inactive for many days, he took only the food and drink of persons in a famine. He moved his household goods out of his house to dramatize the coming desolation of homes in Jerusalem.

For ourselves we may wisely hear from Ezekiel what he said for the gracious God in behalf of the penitent (36:26a): *A new heart I will give you, and a new spirit I will put within you.*

SELECTED READINGS

Exiles of the first captivity are the *rebellious house.*

Ezekiel, like Jeremiah 31:27–34, teaches personal responsibility.

A prophet is to be a watchman   **33:1-11**

In the second stage of his ministry now, Ezekiel's mission is to care tenderly for the Babylonian community.

The people listen but do not heed this son of man   **33:30-33**
God will be a faithful shepherd but administer discipline   **34:1-16**
A vision: the valley of dry bones coming to life   **37:1-23**

The "reborn" will communicate God's blessing to the earth as intended. This famous allegory signifies the nation's restoration.

Beginning and conclusion of Ezekiel's Code   **40:i-4; 48:30-35**

DANIEL

Belteshazzar . . . Shadrach . . . Meshach . . . Abednego

We have lived in a century when persecutions of Jews, even massacres, have been all too frequent. These modern tragedies help us understand the origin and purpose of Daniel. The book appeared about 168–165 B.C. during a persecution. Written by some unknown, Daniel is the hero, not the author.

Antiochus Epiphanes (the terrible) of Syria was ruling Palestine. Enamored of Greek religion, he launched a cruel campaign to uproot Judaism. A statue of Zeus, Greek father of the gods, was set up in the temple where no images were allowed. The forbidden flesh of swine was offered as a mocking sacrifice on the altar. Sacred vessels were looted; sacred books burned. Such a time demanded the unconquerable spirit this book was meant to quicken and did.

Part One (Chapter 1–6) includes six colorful stories about Daniel told in a framework of ancient history. He, called Belteshazzar, with three companions, Shadrach, Meshach, and Abednego, had been taken among the exiles to Babylon. When anti-Semitic King Nebuchadnezzar tries to break their faith they defy him, and are delivered from fire and lions' mouths.

Part Two of the book (Chapters 7–12) includes visions about beasts that stand for kingdoms and horns that stand for kings—of Babylon, Media, Persia, and Greece. But God is a more powerful king than any earthly one. So other kingdoms will fall because all are in the hands of God for justice or mercy. Antiochus and his kingdom, too, will fall.

The book served its purpose. Devoted Jews arose to defend themselves under stouthearted leaders known as Maccabees. After bitter guerrilla warfare they won back Jerusalem and rededicated their desecrated temple on December 25, 165 B.C. They would have a measure of independence until new masters, the Romans, came in 63 B.C. Almost incredible, too, since A.D. 1948 they are at home again, the nation of Israel.

SELECTED READINGS

Daniel and friends refuse Assyrian food; win contest	1:1–21
Shadrach, Meshach, and Abednego survive the fiery furnace	3:1–30
King Belshazzar feasts; a hand writes on the wall; Daniel interprets; a new king, Darius, rises	5:1–31
Daniel prays despite king's decree; is saved from lions	6:1–23
Daniel envisions kingdoms that fall while God's kingdom stands	7:1–14
Daniel prays in confession for his people	9:3–24

God hears and Gabriel brings God's promise of good to come.

HOSEA

How can I hand you over, O Israel! (11:8)

The remaining twelve books in the Old Testament are usually called "minor prophets" but this is unfortunate. Literary works that have lived for 2500 years or more and are still read by hundreds of millions are surely important. Really, "minor" means that the books are brief; "shorter prophetic books" would be a better designation.

The first of the prophets responsible for these books was Amos. He and Hosea ministered to the Northern kingdom with its capital at Samaria. The other ten spoke to Judah, the Southern kingdom. Four—Micah, Zephaniah, Nahum, and Habbakuk— worked between Samaria's fall and Judah's exile. The remaining six prophets appeared during the three centuries after Jerusalem's fall in 587. All are more understandable, interesting, and useful when read in the order of writing shown on page 45.

Hosea's work took place about the year 730 when he was looking at Samaria and Israel only a few years before the destruction of the city and death of the nation. The intolerable moral, religious, and political conditions there had been well described by Amos.

The keynote of Hosea's book is God's love. His revelation grew out of a terrible experience in his own family. He had loved and married Gomer and there were three children, but Gomer became unfaithful. Later, though, she repented and Hosea forgave her. Hosea uses that domestic experience as a living parable. God had "married" Israel but she had been disloyal and the two parties separated. Yet as Hosea had gone on loving Gomer, God wished to win Israel back to himself. Let the people realize God's love, repent and be forgiven.

The Samarians never learned the lesson but continued to be God's faithless ones. They could have turned and lived; they perished. A loving God still longs for responding love from his children and among them, one for another.

SELECTED READINGS

God and Israel are like Hosea and Gomer	1:2–9;3:1–5
The people suffer because they are spiritually ignorant	4:1–6
The people's repentance and love are shallow, worthless	6:1–6
Israel's worship is false; her kings are unworthy	10:1–15
God's love, though spurned, persists	11:1–12
"Return, O Israel, to the Lord your God . . ."	14:1–9

JOEL

I will pour out my spirit on all flesh . . . (2:28)

The books of the prophets are full of dire warnings but also of golden promises. Joel is like that. Although placed so early here among the "shorter prophetic books" this is a rather recent one, possibly written as late as 350 B.C. Concerning the author we know only his name and that he left this small masterpiece.

The Hebrews, now only a small religious community centered around their rebuilt temple, have a plague of locusts. Travellers who have witnessed such a scourge verify Joel's portrayal—darkness as the flying millions blot out the sun, noise that sounds like the cracking of fire, the nakedness of the land after the insects have passed. The author writes, too, about the people's reactions. Old men plan to tell the tale to oncoming generations. Farmers bewail the loss of crops. Priests mourn the lack of meal and wine for offerings. Drunkards lament the wasted vines. Anguished fathers face the pitiable sale of a child to slave-dealers so that the rest of the family may eat.

Joel interprets the event as punishment by the Lord and summons the people to the temple in the words of 2:12–17 which we use as a call to Lenten repentance on Ash Wednesdays. The Lord *had pity*. Then Joel sees the experience as a foretaste of the "day of the Lord" about which former prophets taught. He envisions, too, an outpouring of God's spirit on sons, daughters, old men and young that is now associated with the Pentecostal coming of the Holy Spirit (Acts 2:1–13). Finally the book ends with a picture of Jerusalem, city of peace on holy Mount Zion.

SELECTED READINGS

Everyone laments an invasion by locusts	1:1–12
This plague foreshadows the "day of the Lord"	2:1–11
". . . rend your hearts and not your garments."	2:12–27
The prophet promises that God's spirit will come	2:28,29
God will bring judgment on nations, a new age for Judah	3:19–21

AMOS

But let justice roll down like waters, and righteousness like an everflowing stream. (5:24)

This is the first book of prophetic literature to be produced, just as Amos, whose name it bears, was the first literary prophet.

About 750 B.C. the Hebrew people were still two kingdoms—Northern and Southern, with capitals respectively at Samaria and Jerusalem. Amos was a shepherd who pastured his flocks on the hills of Judah near Tekoa, the village where he had been born. Travellers today visit the windswept and rockstrewn place, a few miles south of Bethlehem, just because Amos lived there.

So Amos was a Southerner who travelled north for a ministry of social reform and religious reformation. By outward appearance Israel seemed to be thriving. Yet the prophet knew that her moral and religious foundations were rotten. In particular, the upper classes were guilty of outrageous greed, spectacular luxury, and cruel oppression of lower classes. Besides, the nation was in the path of Assyrian armies who would sooner or later be rolling westward to engulf her.

The keynote of Amos is righteousness that emphasizes social justice. His best known verse, one of the most frequently quoted from the Bible, is the demand (5:24) that justice be like a mighty waterfall and righteousness be like a stream that never dries up—this in a land where water was scarce.

A few years later Hosea would teach Israel that God is love and his children should be as loving as their Father. Amos' righteousness is not complete without Hosea's love. Equally true, so-called love without that other ingredient, is only romance.

Amos was a hopeful man. Yet in five visions with which the book closes, he sees only a ruined nation, wrecked temple, and slaughtered or captive people. This was the historical event: Assyrian armies came in 721, razed Samaria, took away her population, and none ever returned.

SELECTED READINGS

Amos and his times, about 750 in Israel, the North	1:1,2
God will punish surrounding nations	1:3–5;2:4,5

Two examples: Damascus and the sister kingdom, Judah.

There is doom for Samaria, too	2:6–16
Israel has had many warnings, "Prepare to meet your God."	4:6–17
Seek God, hate evil, love good, and live	5:14–15
God wants goodness and justice, not ceremonies	5:21–24
There is dissolute luxury amid bitter poverty	6:1–8

OBADIAH

*. . . you should not have rejoiced over the people of Judah
in the day of their ruin . . . (verse 12b)*

This shortest prophetic book brings a living message out of a
fascinating, though complicated, bit of history.

Abraham's descendants were three families, often hostile
toward each other. In the times about which Obadiah writes,
certainly long after 587, the warring sons of Jacob, Esau, and
Ishmael were respectively Israelites, Edomites, and Nabateans.
Obadiah himself is an Israelite pouring out his wrath upon the
Edomites. For these sons of Esau had not helped Jacob's sons
when Nebuchadnezzar sacked Jerusalem.

The tables will be turned, says Obadiah in a cry of vengeance.
Nabatean sons of Ishmael will rise against Edomites; then, the
prophet happily declares to the unbrotherly sons of Esau (verse
4) *Though you soar aloft like the eagle, though your nest is
among the stars . . . I will bring you down, says the Lord.*

The Edomites were living in lofty mountains eastward from
Jerusalem. The "eagle's nest" was likely a village on the site of
what are now the ruins of Petra, called "a rose-red city, half as
old as time."

To complete the history, the Nabateans did bring down (312
B.C.) the Edomites; later, too, the Nabateans were brought down.

Readers of Obadiah must ponder a lesson on unbrotherliness.

SELECTED READINGS

One would, naturally, read the whole short book.

JONAH

And should not I pity Nineveh . . . ? (4:11)

Jonah is a tract on racial relations; a sermon on the love of
God who wishes sinners to repent and be forgiven; a parable

that condemns narrow patriotism and appeals for world friendship; an argument for supporting Christianity's world mission. Debating its character as history instead of "parable" obscures such noble teaching and makes a zoological problem out of its symbolic "whale" that is likely only a symbol for Babylon, place of the exile.

The book's name comes from the story's hero, not its author. The date was likely long after 612 B.C. when the Jews had been suffering centuries of abuse at the hands of other nations. We can understand that some had become narrow nationalists lacking love for other peoples. The book was a subtle effort to counter that Hebrew exclusiveness.

For us it is somewhat of an Old Testament forerunner of Christ's parable of the Lost (or Prodigal) Son. The story is told as if it had happened before Nineveh fell in 612 B.C. As it goes, God called Jonah to go there and preach against its wickedness; perhaps its people would repent and God could forgive them. But how could a Hebrew go to preach for such a purpose in that capital city of his nation's mortal enemies? Jonah took ship for Tarshish, the most distant place known in the opposite direction.

What happened on the voyage is familiar enough: Jonah's encounter with a great fish. What followed is the lesson that gets lost in the smog that lies over verses 1:11–2:10.

Jonah had a second call. This time, going to Nineveh as directed, he made a three-day journey across the city declaring (3:4) *Yet forty days and Nineveh shall be overthrown!* Jonah's preaching had unexpected results. The people and the king repented; even the animals joined in the cry for pardon. In his boundless mercy, God withheld his judgment.

Narrow bigot that Jonah was, he was so disappointed that he wanted to die. He had even built himself a booth on a hilltop where he could watch Nineveh writhing in its calamity.

There God taught Jonah a lesson still so grievously needed. God *appointed a plant* to shade Jonah from the burning sun; then he *appointed a worm* to wither the plant. Jonah was angry with God again; it was cruel for him to destroy anything so valuable as that plant. But, had Jonah not wanted God to destroy a city filled with human beings, *more than a hundred and twenty thousand* children infinitely more precious than a mere vine?

SELECTED READINGS
It will be best to read the book omitting this time 1:11–2:10 and concentrating on the precious teaching values elsewhere.

MICAH
He has showed you, O man, what is good . . . (6:8)

This prophet was a peasant farmer who taught in Isaiah's times. He would have known in his own life the injustice that persons of his class were suffering. According to Chapter 3 there are those who *tear the skin from off my people. . . .* Rulers *abhor justice and pervert all equity. . . .* Politicians *give judgment for a bribe . . .* priests *teach for hire . . .* prophets *divine for money. . . .*

Yet Micah includes the usual prophetic promise for restoration. He gives us the portrait of the happy man (4:4) sitting *under his vine and under his fig tree. . . ,* also that figure of peace (4:3): swords beaten into ploughshares and spears into pruning hooks. It is he who envisions the ruler to be born in Bethlehem, who *. . . shall stand and feed his flock . . . and they shall dwell secure. . . .*

Micah had been preceded by Amos and Hosea and may have known First Isaiah. He brings together the key messages from those great prophets in 6:1–8. The passage is a dramatic poem with its scene in a great outdoor courtroom. The mountains are judges; God is plaintiff; the people are defendants. The prophet, as bailiff, calls up the case. God presents his charge: the people have forgotten his gracious mercies and neglected his high purposes. They realize their guilt and plead for mercy. The mountain judges render the verdict that is called "the ideal of true religion" (6:8): *He has showed you, O man, what is good; and what does the Lord require of you but to do justice, and to love kindness, and to walk humbly with your God.*

NAHUM

. . . they will be cut off and pass away. (1:12a)

This book of only three chapters, hidden away near the end of the Old Testament, gets scant attention. Yet in masterful war poetry the author has left a message that the nations need to heed still. God is able to work his justice; tyranny is suicide and those who live by the sword will perish by it.

Neither love nor even pity is featured in the book. Assyria had been hated as perhaps no other nation ever was. Nahum seems to have been writing not long before 612 B.C. when her capital, Nineveh, would be left for what it is now, a mound of earth.

A Jewish patriot then sings these taunting songs with one eye on the welcome catastrophe and the other on a still more welcome deliverance from the oppressor. A first poem celebrates the nature of God whom his people can trust to deal with their wicked enemy. The second and third poems are vivid pictures of the siege and death pangs of Nineveh. The poet exults in a concluding epitaph for Nineveh (3:18, 19): *Your shepherds are asleep, O King of Assyria; your nobles slumber. Your people are scattered on the mountains with none to gather them.*

SELECTED READINGS

It will be possible to savor the full, though bitter, flavor of the book only by reading all of it.

HABAKKUK

. . . but the righteous shall live by his faith. (2:4b)

Habakkuk seems to have been a young man living perhaps fifteen or twenty years before Jerusalem's fall. Nahum had forecast the end of Assyria and her cruelties; a herald would appear on Jerusalem's eastern hilltops to announce *good tidings* of peace. The herald appeared; Assyrians had been conquered by Babylonians. Yet the Hebrews would soon or late be overtaken by Babylonians. As the prophet watches the fearful drama unfolding he is ready to cry out to God: "Why don't you do something about the sufferings of your people?"

Other prophets, denouncing the Hebrews' sins, had taught that their enemies were God's instruments of chastisement. Habakkuk could not accept that answer to his question. So, into his agonizing came this other answer (2:4): *the righteous shall live by his faith.*

The righteous: one who is in right relations with himself, his neighbors, and his God.

Shall live: with all the meaning that the word can have— abundant, victorious, endless existence in well-being.

By faith: trustful belief in faithful friends, parents, children, servants, trust in a faithful self and faithful God.

Imagine now an older Habakkuk wandering in the streets of besieged Jerusalem about 587 B.C. Battle and the chaos of defeat swirl around him. Yet he declares the faith by which he will still live (3:17–18): *Though the fig tree do not blossom, nor fruit be on the vines . . . yet I will rejoice in the Lord. . . .*

SELECTED READINGS

Read it all, not missing 2:4, which for some is an outstanding verse in the Bible, and the concluding glorious psalmic verses.

ZEPHANIAH

A day of wrath is that day . . . (1:15a)

The prophet Zephaniah appears in religious art as a man with a lamp in his hand. The symbolism stems from verse 12 of the first chapter where the Lord is seen searching the streets for persons who deserve to be punished. The culprits are skeptics who think that religion does not matter. As they say, *The Lord will not do good; nor will he do ill* . . . (1:12).

The book likely originated in the 620s and 610s, Jeremiah's time. This suggests that Zephaniah was living when a folk-migration of Scythians in search of a new home passed near Jerusalem and struck terror in Hebrew hearts.

More serious, though, the real menace was Judah's moral and religious condition. The prophet reproaches (3:3, 4) officials who are *roaring lions*, judges who are *wolves*, prophets who are *faithless men*, priests who *profane what is sacred.*

Credited with being the first of the apocalyptic writers, Zephaniah is most noted for his teaching about the "day of the Lord"—somewhat like our concept of Judgment Day. We sing a hymn that grew out of his words about that day: Day of wrath! Day of mourning!

The book of Zephaniah can be taken with Rev. 3:15–17 as a warning to lax and lazy churches. God is in earnest about his plans for humanity. He cannot use faltering nations, churches, or persons.

SELECTED READINGS

The great "day of the Lord" is coming upon the earth   1:7–16
Woe to Jerusalem with her wicked officials, judges, prophets, and priests though a humble remnant will survive   3:1–13
"Sing aloud, O daughter of Zion . . . I will bring you home."   3:14–20

HAGGAI

Because of my house that lies in ruins . . . (1:9b)

Haggai had been one of the younger members of the Jewish community in exile. His work in Jerusalem was done about 520 B.C.

When the returning exiles arrived they started to replace the temple but Haggai in Babylon learned that the work had halted. He decided to go and arouse Judah. He challenged the laggards with his question (1:4): *Is it a time for you yourselves to dwell in your paneled houses while this house lies in ruins?* Zechariah came, too, and helped to speed the work. In 516, twenty years after the first returnees had arrived, a house for God stood on the ancient site. A psalmist could say at its dedication, as we say when dedicating our "temples" (Ps. 84:1): *How lovely is thy dwelling place, O Lord of hosts!*

SELECTED READINGS

The book can be read best according to the possible order of Haggai's speaking: 1:1–11; 2:10–23; 1:15b–2:9; 1:12–15a.

ZECHARIAH

I will . . . dwell in the midst of Jerusalem . . . (8:3)

The book called Zechariah is really two books "bound together": First Zechariah, Chapters 1 through 8; Second Zechariah, 9 through 14. We can think of the first as *The Autobiography of Zechariah the Prophet*. He ministered with Haggai urging the repatriated people of Jerusalem to finish their new temple. His method is to try kindling hope for peace and glory in the city. Its streets, as he envisions them (8:5), will be full of boys and girls playing. Chapter 8 (20–22) closes with the prophet's description of an international processional in the city: *Many peoples . . . shall come to seek the Lord of hosts.*

A reader who reaches Chapter 9 will enter another historical and literary climate. This "book" could be called *Hope: Prophecies from the Late Centuries before Christ*. Perhaps portions were composed as late as the Greek period beginning near 320.

Here (9:9) is the verse in which the prophet sees his nation receiving a sovereign who will be triumphant and victorious but as a humble soul and man of peace. According to Matt. 21:5 Jesus, by his symbolic action on the first Palm Sunday was announcing himself as the one Zechariah had meant.

MALACHI

Have we not all one father? (2:10a)

This prophet, with the pen-name meaning "My Messenger"
must have ministered in Jerusalem about 400 B.C. The community's bright hopes have faded and roseate dreams have become
drab reality. Parts of the book are like a catechism of questions
and answers that reveal the unhappy conditions (2:17):

> The Prophet: *You have wearied the Lord with your words.*
> The People: *How have we wearied him?*
> The Prophet: *By saying, "Everyone who does evil is good in
> the sight of the Lord. . . ." Or by asking, "Where is the
> God of justice?"*

Even the priests are skeptical. They sacrifice blind, lame, and
sick animals on the altars where only the best should be offered
to God. *Present that,* says the prophet (1:8), *to your governor;
will he be pleased with you . . . ?* As for lay people, God's messenger denounces them for half-hearted worship, lax family life,
careless religious teaching, and loose morals.

God cares for them but they cannot enter into the abundance
of his grace until they repent and turn from their evil ways. Let
them trust God's love and be faithful to him.

There is a "book of remembrance" of those who have "feared the Lord and thought on his name." 3:16–18

"I have loved you," says the Lord. That word in Malachi's second verse is a fitting bond between Old Testament and New Testament. Thirty-nine Old Testament books have declared God's grace to Israel. We turn over the last page to read of God's love as it is more fully revealed in the good news of Jesus Christ in the New Testament's twenty-seven books.

Books of the Apocrypha/ Deuterocanonical Books

Fifteen additional books appear at this place in many Bibles, including the recent Common Bible. It is said that all were written during the last two centuries before Christ and the first Christian century. The fifteen books are named:

Tobit	Letter of Jeremiah
Judith	Prayer of Azariah and the Song
Additions to Esther	the three Young Men
Wisdom	Susanna
Sirach (Ecclesiasticus)	Bel and the Dragon
Baruch	1 Maccabees
1 Esdras	2 Maccabees
2 Esdras	The Prayer of Manasseh

While these books are not used by all religious groups, they have their values. The books of 1 and 2 Maccabees add to the Old Testament history and biography; Sirach is much like Proverbs and the Prayer of Manasseh is reminiscent of Ps. 51; there are wholesome teachings in Wisdom.

Between the Testaments

Following the history reported in the Old Testament there was what is called an intertestamental period. The Maccabean struggle, which gave rise to the book of Daniel, ended with Jewish

independence until the Romans came in 63 B.C. Emperor Octa-
vius ruled as Caesar Augustus when Christ was born and New
Testament history began.

Through the intervening years the Jews had clung to their
faith against terrific odds. They were also continuing to develop
the religion we meet in New Testament pages—including synagogue, scribe, Pharisee, temple, law, sabbath ritual and tradition,
exclusion of Gentiles. Meantime their ancient hope had lived. If
Jews would remain faithful to God and his purpose, he would
use Israel for his blessing. Christians believe the hope has become fact in the kingdom of Jesus Christ.

NEW
TESTAMENT

How the New Testament Came To Be

Origins of New Testament books reflect the nature of the lands, peoples, and times out of which they came in the first century after Christ. The world in which the books arose surrounded the Mediterranean Sea at whose eastern end was Palestine, now Israel, where Jesus had lived and ministered.

Palestine's population included a few Samaritans with Gentile Greeks and Romans among the Jews. A majority likely were poor, their homes and clothing plain; many, it seems, were sick, lame, or blind. Men tended orchards and gardens, fished, herded sheep, worked at construction, were merchants, priests, or teachers. Women were busy with the typical household tasks and child rearing. There were synagogues and the temple as centers for education and worship.

Political conditions were disturbed. Roman officials like Pilate, with native underlings such as the Herods, ruled Palestine. Very important for early Christian literature, Jewish revolt brought a Roman army to besiege Jerusalem and in A.D. 70 to ravage the city and destroy the temple. Many Palestinian Jews then joined brethren in little colonies elsewhere in the empire. Paul had earlier undertaken evangelistic work in those little Jewish groups but when they opposed him he had turned to the Gentiles for whom, chiefly, he wrote his epistles.

The Gospels began, of course, with oral tradition as people told what they had heard, seen, or thought about Christ's life, teachings, and significance. Yet the time came when the young church, radiant but imperilled, needed still other books for such needs as these which the biblical authors meant to meet and for which their books can be used today:

That Christ be known and served as Savior and Lord.
That the Spirit's operations result in effective work.
That members for the church be won, sustained, and nurtured.
That Christians have support for loyalty when under attack.
That doctrine be clarified and kept sound.
That personal beliefs and moral ideals be formed and issue in abundant faith-life.

While it would seem that Matthew, printed first in our Bibles, might have been the first biblical book produced, the fact is that all Paul's epistles had been written before any Gospel. So First Thessalonians was the first of all, dating from about A.D. 50. Matthew was not even the first Gospel; that was Mark, probably written about A.D. 65. Certain other books came later than the Gospels, but all New Testament writing had been completed by the end of the half century A.D. 50–100 or possibly a little later.

After each manuscript had been written it was copied and re-copied. Canonization, the selection of the present 66 books as the accepted scriptures for the church, was completed about A.D. 400. Translations into other languages began early. The first printed English New Testament, William Tyndale's, appeared about 1525. The most widely used Bible now is likely the King James version of 1611 but the Revised Standard Version (RSV) of 1952 is supplanting it. Since 1973 we have the Common Bible, an "ecumenical edition" of the RSV with the New Testament revised in 1971.

Books of Christian History and Biography

Historical and biographical material fills half the New Testament's pages. The chief books of it are the Gospels. These four provide a composite life of Christ.

However, the major purpose of New Testament writers was religious, not historical. So, for many, the uppermost value in the Gospels is their teaching about the significance of Christ's person and work, "the gospel in the Gospels." "Gospel," in this sense, is the "good news" or "glad tidings" of what God in Christ graciously did, is doing, and will do for man's salvation through faith. Paralleling this material, too, the Gospels provide the great body of teachings for life and work, such as those in the Sermon on the Mount and thirty or more parables which are choice "go, be, and do" lessons.

Yet, along with that good news gospel and those other teachings, the Gospels contain typical history and biography—narratives of Christ's birth and childhood, records of his years of public ministry and events of his passion, resurrection, and afterward. Mingled with these are accounts of his compassionate deeds of miracle-working. There are also accounts of the lives and works of his disciples, with others around them. All this makes everything come alive and be meaningful for the present scene.

Matthew, Mark, Luke, and John are entitled "The Gospel According To . . ." because they tell that good news of Jesus Christ —good news as he reveals it in person, work, and word, especially about the salvation that is to be had in him. The first three "see together" so largely that they are called "synoptic Gospels." While much of their contents is similar, each reveals the identity of an author, offers additional facts and insights, has elements unique enough to give it a special character and particular service to render. John is quite different, not so much a narrative of events as an interpretation that lifts high the significance of Christ for faith-life.

We cannot be certain that even one of the four writers of Gospels was acquainted personally with Jesus; possibly John Mark had seen him. Yet they had heard the spoken word from earliest Christians who were remembering the facts they had found most helpful! Perhaps, too, "shorter gospels" had been written before our four. Scholars think Matthew and Luke used such materials and also quoted broadly from Mark. Some also teach that the thinking, experiences, and concerns of early church persons is reflected in these writings.

It may be said of all the Gospels, as John said of his (20:31): *These are written that you may believe that Jesus is the Christ . . . and that believing you may have life in his name.*

MATTHEW, MARK, and LUKE

. . . the Kingdom of God is at hand, repent and believe in the gospel. (Mark 1:14b)

The Gospel writers repeat each other at many points. As an instance, the miracle of feeding five thousand appears in all four Gospels. So selected readings on Matthew, Mark, and Luke are woven together here for a single, connected story, omitting repetitions. Additional material on John is given later. Correspondingly, the synoptic Gospels are introduced together here; an introduction to John will precede selected readings from that book.

Matthew appears as the first Gospel in our Bibles although it was neither the first New Testament book nor even the first Gospel to be completed. There are other reasons for the place it holds. One reason is that Matthew is a fitting bridge between Old Testament and New. The author seems to have been a Christian Jew who was especially eager to tell his own people about God's gift to them. More than sixty Old Testament quotations show this interest. However, according to this evangelist, Jesus is God's gift to others as well as Jews.

As another reason for this Gospel's position in the New Testament, Matthew can be called the gospel of teachings. It suits the aim which the author suggests when he quotes Jesus' great commission: *Go . . . make disciples . . . teaching. . . .* With an interesting habit of putting things together in collections, he includes five groups of teachings, chiefly the Sermon on the Mount (Chapters 5, 6, and 7). The major theme of the teachings is the nature of the Kingdom of God (because of his Jewish concern the author says "kingdom of heaven" to avoid speaking outright the name of God) and the life of a citizen in it. This book can be the chief laboratory manual of Christians for the experiences of living in that new community as it breaks into history.

The Gospel's name leads people naturally to think it was written by the man in the tax office when Jesus said (Matt. 9:9) *Follow me.* However, Bible scholars believe that the book was written by someone else. There is that prevailing view that the synoptic Gospels had ancestors. So, this Gospel's writer quoted from a collection of teachings made by the real Matthew and gave that man's name to the work. As a result the author is most often said to have been some Christian teacher working in Antioch of Syria about A.D. 80.

Whoever wrote Matthew, whenever and wherever, he composed what some have called "the greatest book in the world." It is used in church schools more than any other book of the Bible.

Mark, in a way, is Simon Peter's Gospel although that apostle did not write it. Peter had visited Rome to strengthen the Roman congregation. Suddenly, though, he was taken away from them to be a martyr. What happened next is told in an ancient manuscript: "Mark, having been the interpreter of Peter, wrote down accurately everything he remembered." Because Peter spoke in his native tongue of Aramaic, he had needed someone to turn his words into the Romans' language. The interpreter, it seems, was the John Mark who wrote this Gospel after Peter's martyrdom, usually dated about A.D. 64. This Gospel, then, was the first written.

Mark was well equipped for his writing in other ways. He had travelled with Paul and Barnabas to Cyprus on the first missionary journey, probably A.D. 46–48. He served Paul later, too, and is mentioned in Second Timothy (4:11). Further, there is a tradition that the *young man* present at the arrest in Gethsemane, and mentioned in verse 14:51, may have been Mark himself. If so, this evangelist is the one who may have seen Jesus in the flesh.

This first of the Gospels to be written is also the shortest and simplest. Perhaps that is why many readers like it best. There is another reason for its popularity. "Immediately," appears nine times in the first chapter alone. Thus, brief and action-packed, Mark's is the gospel of deeds. Jesus here is the Great Worker advancing the kingdom of God among men.

Luke, the third Gospel in the New Testament is the first of two volumes by the author: The Gospel According to Luke and The Acts of the Apostles. The twofold work is the most important history ever written.

Here we read first an introduction to Luke's complete history (1:1–4). He is writing for Theophilus, possibly a Roman official and a patient of this physician. It is as if Theophilus had asked, "What about this new religion spreading through the empire?"

Luke wants the inquirer to have an accurate report on Christ and the church. He proceeds according to proper methods of historical research. He has (1:2, 3) *followed closely all things for some time past* and has consulted *eyewitnesses and ministers of the word.* We know that Luke had been in Palestine where he could talk with older people who had known the Lord—possibly Mary. He had been a companion of Paul. He also incorporated in his Gospel a large proportion of Mark's book. So Theophilus was carried back closely and reliably to the events about which Luke writes and happily we can look over his shoulder as he reads.

The beloved physician, as Paul calls him (Col. 4:14) had likely settled down at medical practice in Ephesus, now in southwestern Turkey. There, where so much biblical literature was produced, he wrote possibly in A.D. 80 or 90. As an educated man Luke writes with care and precision. It is his book which includes among his birth narratives those four poems used in church liturgies. One writer calls this "the most beautiful of all books."

Luke's can be called the Gospel for humanity, our prime source for humane teaching values. Luke has filled it with people, women and children as well as men, Jews and Gentiles of many types. And always, in the center of the picture is the Lord of all, making it possible (as Luke says in 3:6) for *all flesh* to *see the salvation of God.*

We are particularly indebted to Luke for a portion of Christ's ministry reported by him alone, 9:51–18:14, nearly half of the book. Here is that favorite parable, the Good Samaritan. Here also is the famous fifteenth chapter with the Master Storyteller's unforgettable parable of the loving father with two sons—one loyal but bitter, the other wayward but repentant. Mankind will everlastingly take hope in the joy of that father whom Jesus lets speak in the manner of the Heavenly Father (15:22, 24): *Bring quickly the best robe and put it on him . . . for this my son was dead, and is alive again; he was lost, and is found.*

SELECTED READINGS (Matthew, Mark, Luke)

Part One: Christ's Early Life

Why and how Luke wrote his Gospel | Luke 1:1–4
An angel announces Jesus' birth to Mary | Luke 1:26–38
John the Baptist is born and named | Luke 1:57–80

This second of the four poems by Luke, used in services of worship, is called the Benedictus.

The Christ-child is born in Bethlehem | Luke 2:1–7

The story is told also in Matt. 1:18–25. Due to an ancient mistake in counting we must say the date is between 6 and 4 B.C.

Angels announce the birth; shepherds visit the babe | Luke 2:8–20

The angels' song, Luke's third poem, is our Gloria in Excelsis.

Eastern "wise men" arrive in Bethlehem with gifts | Matt. 2:1–12

The men were Persians, priestly scholars. Herod the Great is the native tyrant who ruled Palestine for Rome, 40 to 4 B.C.

The family flees to Egypt | Matt. 2:13–23
Jesus is a Passover pilgrim to Jerusalem | Luke 2:41–52

After eighteen unreported years he will take up public ministry.

John the Baptist baptizes in the Jordan River | Mark 1:5, 6
John preaches boldly for repentance and its fruits | Luke 3:7–14

In Isaiah's words (40:3) he is a voice crying . . . *in the wilderness prepare the way of the Lord.*

Jesus is baptized; the Holy Ghost witnesses | Mark 1:9–11
Jesus meets temptation victoriously | Matt. 4:1–11

He could have been a popular benefactor, wonder-worker, or earthly king. As a suffering servant Messiah he will minister in the Father's way for the kingdom of God.

Part Two: Christ's Public Ministry

Section A: Christ's Early Teaching, Preaching, Healing in Galilee

Writers mention: earlier Judean ministry (according to John), this Galilean ministry, Perean ministry (according to Luke), later Judean ministry. The time was likely three years.

Jesus preaches repentance, the kingdom's presence, and belief in the Gospel | Mark 1:14, 15

Kingdom means two things: God's realm or domain; God's reign or rule. It is here and now; its fullness is to be then and there. "Kingdom of God" is "kingdom of heaven" in Matthew.

Jesus speaks his "good news" in the hometown synagogue of Nazareth; old neighbors reject him   Luke 4:16–30

He describes his mission in Isaiah's words (61:1, 2).

Peter, Andrew, James, and John are called as disciples following a great catch of fish   Matt. 4:18–22

Jesus teaches, preaches, and heals in Capernaum   Mark 1:21–45

Here we meet some of the more than thirty miracle narratives. They are always to be read with the inquiry, "What does this teach me about the relations of God and man?"

> a. Teaching in the Capernaum synagogue; exorcising an unclean spirit; healing Peter's mother-in-law; others (Mark 1:21–34). New Testament people often thought of the sick, especially mentally ill, as possessed by a demon serving Satan.
>
> b. Leaving Capernaum to preach in other villages (Mark 1:35–39). It seems that Jesus was more deeply concerned about ministering to human spirits than to physical bodies.

Section B: Christ's Popularity among the People and the Rise of Hostility among Jewish Leaders

Even early in his ministry Christ gained foes as well as friends. He pleased the common people; they were ready to accord him the reverence due to God. Religious and political leaders, fearful if not jealous, decided early to destroy him.

Jesus heals a paralyzed man carried by four friends; scribes and Pharisees declare him a blasphemer   Luke 5:17–26

Levi (Matthew), tax collector, is called to follow   Luke 5:27–32

He gives a feast with Jesus as a guest. Enemies disapprove the company the Lord keeps.

The Pharisees fault the disciples for plucking grain on the Sabbath; Jesus declares the day was made for man   Mark 2:23–28

Comparison with the commandment (Exod. 20:8–11) is instructive.

Jesus cures a man with a withered hand on the sabbath; enemies decide to do away with him **Mark 3:1–6**
By tradition, medical treatment on the sabbath was permissible only in cases of life or death.

Section C: Christ's Choosing of Twelve; his Sermon on the Mount

The twelve are chosen to be disciples and apostles **Mark 3:13–19**
They are to *be with him* as disciples, learners, followers; they are also to *be sent out* as apostles, witnesses, workers for him.

The Sermon on the Mount **Matt. 5:1–7:29**
(There is a "sermon on the plain" in Luke 6:20b–49.)
Jesus deals with the theme: Citizens of God's Kingdom: His Providences for Them and Their Responsibilities to Him.
    a. Introduction to the collection of teachings and the nine Beatitudes—citizens' ways to blessedness and corresponding destinies (5:1–12):
        (1) Spirituality: citizenship in God's realm; (2) suffering: comfort; (3) humility: inheritance of the earth; (4) goodness: satisfaction as to righteousness; (5) merciful helpfulness: mercy from fellowmen; (6) integrity: vision of God; (7) peacemaking: sonship of the Father; (8) sacrifice: rule by the king; (9) discipleship: heavenly reward.
    b. Citizens' purposes in the world: salt and light (5:13–16).
    c. Citizens' use of scriptures: doing and teaching *these commandments* (5:17–19).
    d. Citizens' righteousness that *exceeds* (5:20–6:18). A citizen of God's kingdom is not to be like a scribe or Pharisee. Two phases of superior behavior are described:
        (1) maximum morality versus only obeying law, with five examples and a summary (5:21–48): (a) being reconciled instead of just refraining from murder; (b) being chaste instead of just abstaining from adultery; (c) being honorable instead of just keeping an oath; (d) being kindly instead of just getting even; (e) loving even enemies instead

of loving just friends; summary: being perfect as the Father is.

(2) real religion versus only profession, summary with three examples (6:1–18): summary, sincere devotion; examples, (a) doing charity privately versus display in giving; (b) having quiet fellowship with God versus making outward show in prayer—The Lord's Prayer; (c) practicing secret self-discipline versus public demonstration when fasting.

e. Citizens' "highest good," principle and promise (6:19–34). (1) The principle, seek first God's kingdom and righteousness, with four examples: (a) Strive for spiritual versus material treasures. (b) Have a *sound* eye versus one *not sound*. (c) Serve God only versus *God and Mammon*. (d) Care for eternal life versus worrying over temporal externals.

(2) The promise: *and all these things shall be yours. . . .*

f. Citizens' principle of "similar returns" (7:1–12). How the Golden Rule operates in (1) judging; (2) giving; (3) getting.

g. Citizens' lives and deeds (7:13–23), illustrated in contrasts: (1) two ways of entrance; (2) two kinds of teachers; (3) two kinds of disciples—citizens' deeds are to match their words.

h. Citizens' helps (7:24–29): (1) secure foundations in Christ; (2) a teacher with authority.

Section D: Christ's Parables of the Kingdom, Sending Forth of the Twelve, and the Transfiguration

Jesus teaches about the kingdom and its citizens in nine parables
Matt. 13:1–52; Mark 4:26–29

There are more than thirty parables in the Gospels—stories told about natural things to teach spiritual truths. These are nine brave words about the nature, growth, and worth of the kingdom and citizenship in it. God's power is in action in the world; the drama of redemption is invincibly moving on, act by act and scene by scene:

a. Soils, with explanation and reason (Matt. 13:1–23)

b. Weeds, with explanation (Matt. 13:24–30; 13:36–43)

c. Flourishing mustard seed; lively yeast (Matt. 13:44–52)

d. Hidden treasure, pearl of great value; net; treasures old and new (Matt. 13:44–52)

e. Virile seed and fertile earth (Mark 4:26–29)

Jesus calms a storm on the Galilean lake   Mark 4:35–41
Jesus heals Jairus' daughter   Luke 8:40–42,49–56
Christ instructs twelve to minister for him   Matt. 9:35–11:1

The disciples are learning to be the apostles they will become.

a. Plight of the people; the twelve sent out (Matt. 9:35–10:4)

b. Instructions for the journey (Matt. 10:5–15)

c. Expected persecution and fearless witness (Matt. 10:16–33)

d. Costs and rewards of undivided service (Matt. 10:34–11:1)

John the Baptist is martyred by Herod and Herodias   Mark 6:14–29
Jesus travels "abroad"; heals a gentile's daughter   Mark 7:24–30
Peter declares "you are the Christ . . . "   Matt. 16:13–20

For the first time a disciple names Jesus as the Anointed, Messiah, King. Simon is called Peter, the rock man—with the new faith his foundation is on rock, not sand. From this point, like a watershed in the Gospels, the Lord speaks often of his suffering, death, and resurrection.

Jesus teaches on cross-bearing and finding life   Luke 9:23–27
The transfiguration takes place   Luke 9:28–36

Now the disciples knew Christ as God at work for men and worthy to be followed as Lord.

The disciples dispute who is greatest; Jesus teaches childlike humility, concern for the young, and self-denial; gives the parable of ninety and nine   Matt. 18:1–14

Section E: Christ's Further Work, Reported Largely by Luke Alone

Luke opens the section by saying (9:51), *When the days drew near for him to be received up, he set his face to go to Jerusalem.* This the Lord does despite the peril ahead.

Jesus tells the parable of the Good Samaritan   Luke 10:25–37
To remember: Samaritans and Jews were not loving neighbors.

Jesus visits Mary and Martha in Bethany and commends Mary's
personal devotion   Luke 10:38–42
Jesus gives a parable of a foolish rich man   Luke 12:13–21
Three parables on God's seeking and saving grace   Luke 15:1–32
One of the Bible's greatest chapters. Who has not heard grate-
fully about the lost sheep (15:1–7), the lost coin (15:8–10), the
lost (or "prodigal") son (15:11–32)?

Ten lepers are healed; only one gives thanks   Luke 17:11–19
Proud Pharisee and humble tax-collector contrasted   Luke 18:9–14

Section F: Christ's Final Approach to Jerusalem

"Let the children come to me . . ."   Mark 10:13–16
Children have the essential kingdom characteristics of unques-
tioning trust, steadfast loyalty, and true love.

" . . . what must I do to inherit eternal life?"   Mark 10:17–22
When a rich man refuses to become a disciple, Jesus cites the
perils of wealth.

Jesus corrects worldy ambitions of disciples   Mark 10:35–45
Rich Zaccheus, tax-collector, receives Jesus   Luke 19:1–10
Jesus turns toward Jerusalem for the last time   Luke 19:28

Part Three: Christ's Passion and Resurrection

Christians have been stirred most of all by the events of the
"last week" to which the Gospel writers have devoted a quarter
of their records. In particular, Christians regard the crucifixion
and resurrection as supreme deeds of God for accomplishing his
grace toward mankind and bringing it into closer fellowship with
him and within its own kind.

Section A: Christ's Triumphal Entry and Conflict in Jerusalem

Christ has a week of suffering while he wins the victory in his
earthly work for humanity.

Jesus is acclaimed as he enters Jerusalem   Mark 11:1–11
Jesus cleanses the temple; children praise him   Matt. 21:12–17
Jesus gives the parable of one son who refused but went and one
who promised but did not go   Matt. 21:28–32
Scheming leaders question Jesus   Matt. 22:15–22;22:34–40

Enemies put three questions to trap Jesus and he asks one in
reply. He outsmarts them but they will have their evil way with
him. Two of the questions are cited:

a. By Pharisees and Herodians, about paying taxes to Caesar
(Matt. 22:15–22)
Render proper dues to each, Caesar and God, Christ teaches.
b. By scribes, about the commandments (Matt. 22:34–40)
Here Christ combines two Old Testament teachings (Deut.
6:4, 5 and Lev. 19:18) for the "great commandment."

Jesus denounces pretenses of his opponents   Matt. 23:1–39
Jesus praises a poor widow's precious offering   Mark 12:41–44
Jesus speaks on the future   Mark 13:1–37; Matt. 25:1–46

Even in Old Testament times prophets and people were expect-
ing *a day of the Lord* that would bring such a judgment as Jesus
describes. The Lord names human attitudes and acts important
in a "judgment day"; faithfulness, preparedness, and helpfulness.

a. Times and signs: destruction of Jerusalem; close of the
age; coming of the Son of Man; the judgment (Mark 13:1–
37)
A generation later, Jerusalem was indeed destroyed by troops
under Titus, A.D. 70. Eternal issues hang upon humans' re-
sponses to God's reign and their deeds in his realm.
b. Jesus gives parables of maidens wise or foolish with lamps
and of servants entrusted with talents (Matt. 25:1–30)
c. The great separation in final judgment (Matt. 25:31–46)

For thirty pieces of silver Judas Iscariot plots to aid in the arrest of
Jesus   Luke 22:1–6

Judas' reasons remain a mystery except John's Gospel (12:4–6)
offers one possible explanation: Judas' love of money.

Section B: Christ's Last Supper, Trial, Crucifixion, Ascension
(Additional accounts are given in John beginning at 13:1.)

The twelve have their Last Supper with Jesus	Mark 14:12–25

The first written account of the Lord's Supper can be read in
1 Cor. 11:23–28.

Jesus forewarns Peter and the other disciples	Mark 14:26–31
Jesus prays in Gethsemane	Matt. 26:36–46
Judas betrays him and the Master is arrested	Matt. 26:47-56
Jesus is tried and condemned	Matt. 26:57–27:31

a. Investigated by Jewish authorities; arraigned before Annas
and Caiphas; Peter denies; Jews condemn (Matt. 26:57–
27:1)
The council could not by night invoke the death penalty.
Also that penalty required Roman approval.
b. Charge and examination before Pilate (Matt. 27:2; 11–14)
Christ's enemies are threatening Pilate with a charge of disloyalty to Caesar. Jesus was taken to a hearing by Herod
(Luke 23:6–12) and Judas committed suicide (Matt. 27:3–10)
c. Before Pilate; Barabbas released (Matt. 27:15–26)
Pilate could have released Christ if he had possessed the
courage; even against opposition he did make this weak
effort.
d. The trial ends; Jesus, mocked, is led away (Matt. 27:27–
31)

Jesus is crucified	Luke 23:26–49

Here are three more of the "seven words from the cross"; others
are in Matt. 27 and John 19.

Joseph of Arimathea, and Nicodemus according to John (19:38–42),	
bury Jesus in the former's tomb	Luke 23:50–56

The crucifixion and resurrection have remained central in Christian language, music, art, and architecture—not to speak of teaching and belief. Always though, among Protestants, an empty cross
suggests that there was life beyond the cross. As Christ lives, his
people live and shall live.

"He has risen."   Mark 16:1–8
"Go . . . I am with you always . . ."; the "great commission" to teach
and "make disciples of all nations . . ."   Matt. 28:16–20
Other appearances are cited under selected readings in John.

Jesus ascends   Luke 24:50–53

JOHN

For God so loved the world . . . (John 3:16)

While other Gospels remind a reader of a biography, John's is more like a portrait than a photograph. Showing how Jesus looked to an artist in discipleship, it leaves an indelible impression of who the Person Jesus was and can be for believers. Further, since the author is writing long after the earthly ministry ended, he is writing about the Jesus of Nazareth who had become for Christians the living Christ and abiding presence.

While we do here have facts, as in the other Gospels, we must look especially for meanings. For instance, "life" is such a prominent word throughout John's Gospel that this can be called the gospel of life. The author, of course, is not thinking of physical existence alone. He means what Jesus meant (10:10b): *. . . I came that they may have life, and . . . abundantly.* John often calls it *eternal life*—life boundless in all directions.

Many persons think that this Gospel is the work of the disciple whom Jesus called from fishing on the Sea of Galilee. Now he is very old, they say, living in Ephesus and writing for the Christian community in that region. However, others say we know only that this is some John, writing avout A.D. 100.

While John is a favorite Gospel with many persons, for some it is a difficult book. It may be understood better if viewed as possibly the written remains of a series of sermons. We expect preachers to keep true to the facts but also make the meaning of those facts vivid and compelling. In many ways John's Gospel seems to be the work of a dramatic, inspiring preacher.

John has no parables in his Gospel; there are two allegories:

The Good Shepherd and the Vine and the Branches. Miracles are called *signs*. There are several "discourses"—monologues or long talks by Jesus. Certain narratives, such as washing the disciples' feet, add to the synoptic record. Here, too, we read about that "appearance" on the beach of Galilee where Peter, who denied, now declares his love for the Master and receives the commission he obeyed to martyrdom *Tend my sheep* (21:16).

A tribute one can pay John is to remember the verse 3:16: *For God so loved. . . .* There are also the great "I am's": *. . . Bread of life . . . Light of the World . . . Good Shepherd . . . Resurrection and the Life . . . Way . . . Truth . . . Life . . . True Vine. . . .*

SELECTED READINGS

The prologue to John's Gospel: the coming of Jesus, eternal Word in flesh, brings light, truth, and grace to men   1:1–18
Those eighteen verses are the theme of the whole Gospel; what follows can be viewed as illustrations of it.

John the Baptist declares the "Lamb of God" preeminent   1:19–34
Andrew, Simon, Philip, and Nathaniel become disciples   1:35–51
Jesus gives a "sign" at a wedding in Cana   2:1–11
John calls the miracle a *sign*; it points to some hidden truth.

In Jerusalem Jesus has a night visitor; he and Nicodemus discuss new birth and eternal life   3:1–21
From this event we have the great verse 16 and Christ's teaching on the way of entering the eternal life which John mentions so often. Nicodemus will later defend the Lord before the Sanhedrin (7:50–52) and assist with his burial (19:38–42).

Jesus talks with a woman near Sychar, Samaria   4:1–42
Sychar is about twenty-five miles north of Jerusalem and a mile from Jacob's well. Salvation is not for Jews alone.

    a. Telling the woman about *living water* (4:1–15)
    b. Discussing worship in *spirit and truth* (4:16–26)
    c. Inviting the disciples to the food, that is *in doing the will of God* (4:27–38)

d. Winning Samaritans for the ... *Savior of the world.* ... (4:39–42)

Jesus heals an invalid man at a pool in Jerusalem; Jews deny his equality with the Father 5:1–18

The opposition has begun as John tells it in his Gospel.

Five thousand are fed after the twelve return to Jesus following their early ministering for him 6:1–71

Here is the miracle narrative included in all four Gospels. Here also is the first *I am*.

a. The multitude is fed (6:1–14; Matt. 14:13–21; Mark 6:30–44; Luke 9:10–17)
b. Jesus refuses a crown; walks on the sea; the people seek him (6:15–24)
c. Jesus declares *I am the Bread of Life*; Jews murmur; many disciples *draw back* (6:25–71)

If one's "will is to do his will, he shall know ..." 7:16–24

Confronted by bitter enemies Christ tries to win them as followers.

"I am the Light of the world ..." 8:12–30

Debate in the temple continues. Enemies who do not accept him as Christ, Son of the Father, will *walk in darkness.* ...

Jesus speaks on freedom that comes by the truth 8:31–48
The Good Shepherd is portrayed in an allegory 10:1–18

This first allegory is also about the sheep, the sheepfold, and the door. We remember it best for verse 10:10b about his coming for his people's abundant life.

Jesus raises Lazarus at Bethany 11:1–44

Here, verse 25, *I am the resurrection and the life* is the precious teaching that persons in Christ are never out of life.

A woman of Bethany anoints Jesus and is censured 12:1–11

Believing, as her people had long believed, in the coming of a Messiah, Mary meant to anoint Jesus as that king. Knowing the events about to take place, he sees it as anointing for burial.

Jesus washes the disciples' feet at the Last Supper   13:1–20

We are entering what we remember as Passion Week.

Jesus speaks his "farewell discourses"   13:31–17:26

Christ was striving to instruct and strengthen the disciples for troublous times ahead. These passages are memorable:

    a. *A new commandment* for his little children (13:31–35)
    b. Discussion of faith, hope, love, and obedience (14:1–15); here is the precious (14:1) *Let not your heart be troubled....*
    c. Promise that the Counselor (Holy Spirit) will come (14:16–31)
    d. Allegory of the Vine and the Branches (15:1–11)
    e. Words of comfort for his going away (16:16–33)
    f. Intercessory prayer for unity among his own (17:1–26)

Jesus is crucified on Calvary   19:17–30

Here are the last of "the last seven words."

Joseph of Arimathea and Nicodemus bury the Lord's' body 19:38–42
Jesus is raised   20:1–18
Jesus appears to disciples in Jerusalem, once with Thomas absent and later with Thomas present   20:19–29

It has been reckoned that there were ten appearances.

John's purpose for his Gospel   20:31
At breakfast with Jesus beside Galilee Peter, who had denied, declares undying love and is restored to favor   21:1–19

Books of Church History and Biography

All New Testament books are, to some degree, books of history and biography. The Gospels are prominently Christian history and biography; The Acts of the Apostles is specifically church history and biography and remaining books contain some such material.

When was the church born? Persons give differing answers:

when God planned it; at the call of Abraham; at the birth of Christ or his resurrection; at Pentecost; when the first congregation was formed. One's preference depends on his definition of church. We shall say that the church is the continuing ministry of the body of Christ and think of the church's birthday as Pentecost, the event recorded in The Acts 2:1–11. It was a turning point in all history.

After 39 verses of The Acts, in which the risen Christ concludes his earthly presence and Pentecost occurs, the church is being led forward by Peter. Possibly about A.D. 33, the mighty Saul, later to be called Paul, comes on the scene and gradually assumes the principal leadership role. Then the movement, overcoming all the hostility Jesus had predicted, blankets the Mediterranean world during its first generation.

The story of Paul's work is largely the thrilling report of his travels for the Christian mission. These were perilous ventures. In 2 Cor. 11:23–33 the apostle mentions labor, imprisonments, beatings, stonings, shipwreck, hunger and thirst, cold and exposure. The Acts closes with Paul living *at his own expense* in Rome where he had long wanted to be, but as a prisoner of the emperor awaiting trial on false charges of revolutionary activity trumped up by enemies in Jerusalem. Even so, he found it possible to carry on with his evangelistic work. (It is taught by some that Paul had not only the three missionary journeys reported in The Acts but also a fourth; see page 108.)

What happened finally to Paul? Tradition says that he was beheaded where a chapel stands now outside the walls of Rome. Too, certain archaeologists hold that his remains lie under the high altar of the church called St. Paul's Outside the Walls. On a great vault there you can see a rough inscription gouged out of the concrete, meaning, "Paul: Apostle; Martyr."

Called "The Way" by early believers, Christianity spread through (1) Jerusalem and then (2) into all Palestine. Next it extended its reach into (3) Syria and (4) Asia Minor. Finally it arrived in (5) Europe and from there it has covered (6) the world.

THE ACTS OF THE APOSTLES

. . . and you shall be my witnesses in Jerusalem and in all Judea and Samaria and to the end of the earth. (1:8b)

The Acts is Part Two of the two-volume work called Luke-Acts, said earlier to be the most important history ever written. That high evaluation fits particularly this Part Two.

Major facts about the author's life and work were given in the introduction to Luke's Gospel. Briefly, he was a Greek physician writing likely in Ephesus about A.D. 90. He had already told a certain Theophilus about Christ; now he will tell that man about the beginnings of the church. The man knows that Christian congregations exist already in considerable numbers and others are springing up all the way from Jerusalem to Rome. The author will explain this miracle.

Luke first mentions his Gospel as the book in which he had dealt (1:1) *with all that Jesus began to do and teach.* "Began" is significant. In Luke's mind the events of The Acts really began with Christ. The church, under the Holy Spirit's power, is the lengthening and broadening work of the Father through him.

Early in The Acts, here only, is that record of Pentecost when Christ's followers sensed the Holy Spirit's presence with power. Immediately they took up the work that Christ had been doing and the church has ever after been doing in education, evangelism, fellowship, social ministry, stewardship, and worship.

As Luke writes later chapters of The Acts he recounts an epic in which he played a role himself. He was Paul's companion for some years in the apostle's famous missionary journeys. In that connection a unique feature of The Acts appears. After writing in the third person singular, Luke suddenly turns to first person plural. There are four "we-sections" (16:10–18; 20:5–15; 21:1–18; 27:1–28:16) which could be quotations from a diary that Luke kept while traveling with Paul.

SELECTED READINGS

Section A: Earliest beginnings of the Church (Pentecost, A.D. 30)

Luke, the author, introduces his work   1:1–3

Luke also concludes his Gospel as he presents another act in the ongoing "drama of God's purpose for mankind."

Jesus promises the Spirit's coming; commissions disciples to be apostles; ascends from Mount Olivet 1:4–14

The Holy Spirit fills Christ's followers on Pentecost 2:1–11

The Holy Spirit is here! The Jews had this festival occurring fifty days after Passover. Now Pentecost is a Christian festival, too, celebrating the continuous coming of God's Spirit as power that works in and through Christ's people.

Peter preaches a "first Christian sermon"; 3,000 believe; the church thrives with peace, unity, and property in common 2:14–47

Section B: The Church under Peter's Leadership—Development in Jerusalem, Palestine, and Syria (A.D. 30–46)

Peter and John heal a lame beggar at a temple gate 3:1–10

Early Christians kept many of their Jewish customs; as we see, they are observing times of worship in the temple.

Enemies of Christ arrest Peter and John; they defend themselves boldly and are released with a warning 4:1–22

Peter's teaching, preaching, and healing resulted in arrest three times. Yet Peter had once denied knowing the Lord!

Though the Christians' possessions are to be common property, Ananias and Sapphira deceive and perish 4:32–5:11

Seven deacons are appointed to serve tables 6:1–7

They are to do other work so that the apostles can be free for preaching and teaching.

Stephen, first Christian martyr, is stoned to death 7:54–8:1a

Though only a deacon, Stephen had begun to speak for Christ. At the end of this passage (8:1a) the name of Saul, later to be Paul, appears first in The Acts.

Saul, leading persecution, scatters churches' members 8:1b–4

Persecution only serves to spread Christianity!

Philip, evangelist, wins an Ethiopian convert 8:26–40

Christianity has crossed the color barrier and is beginning to become a world religion.

Saul becomes a Christian; begins to work in Syria   9:1–19a

The greatest enemy of the early church will become its greatest missionary. The story of the conversion is also in Acts 22:5–11 and 26:12–18, and the first chapter of Galatians.

Peter baptizes Gentile Cornelius and his household   10:1–48

The mission to Gentiles begins. Peter had been working in such places as Lydda and in Joppa, home of the good Tabitha or Dorcas.

Section C: Paul's First Missionary Journey—Development of the Church in Asia Minor (A.D. 46–48)

Antioch in Syria	Antioch of Pisidia	Iconium
Seleusia	Iconium	Antioch of Pisidia
Salamis	Lystra	Perga
Paphos	Derbe	Attalia
Perga	Lystra	Antioch in Syria

Paul and Barnabas minister in Syrian Antioch   11:19–30

It was then capital of Syria as Damascus is now. The congregation had been founded by refugees from persecution probably led by Saul, Paul.

Herod Agrippa makes James the first apostolic martyr   12:1–5
Antioch Christians send out Paul, Barnabas, and John   13:1–3

This church becomes headquarters for Paul's missionary journeys. This John is likely John Mark, author of the Gospel.

The missionaries visit Salamis and Paphos in Cyprus, Barabas' birthplace; Saul, now Paul, becomes foremost leader in the church 13:4–12
John Mark returns home to Jerusalem; Paul and Barnabas at Antioch in Pisidia "turn to the Gentiles"   13:13–49

The missionaries are on mainland Asia Minor. Paul's habit of going first to a synagogue fails often.

Paul and Barnabas are worshipped as gods in Lystra; the journey ends; they return to Antioch in Syria   14:8–20

Paul will enlist Timothy here on his second journey. It is profitable to study related epistles along with The Acts. The churches of this journey are those to which Paul wrote Galatians.

Church leaders confer in Jerusalem   15:1–21

Gentiles may now join Christian ranks without first becoming Jewish. Christianity becomes a religion in itself, not just a "denomination" in Judaism.

Section D: Paul's Second Missionary Journey: Christianity in Europe (A.D. 49–51)

Antioch in Syria	Troas	Corinth
Syria	Philippi	Ephesus
Cilicia	Thessalonica	Caesarea
Derbe	Berea	Jerusalem
Lystra	Athens	Antioch in Syria

Barnabas and Mark to Cyprus, Paul and Silas to Asia Minor 16:36–41

John Mark will work with Paul later (2 Tim. 4:11). Barnabas, by tradition, gave his life as a martyr in Cyprus.

Timothy joins the party at Lystra; it goes to Troas   16:1–10

Paul is called to cross the bridge to Europe. In verse 10 we have the first use of "we" in Luke's history.

The missionaries entering Europe work first at Philippi; Lydia is baptized and lodges the party   16:11–18

This is Greece; Europe is receiving Christianity! Those who wish to study related epistles may read Philippians now (see page 104).

The church is planted in Thessalonia and Beroea   17:1–13

These cities are now Saloniki and Verreia. The typical trouble arises. This is the time to read the Thessalonian letters. For introductions see page 107.

Silas and Timothy remain behind; Paul goes to Athens   17:14–34

Paul's speech on Mars Hill is one of history's most famous.

Paul ministers eighteen months at Corinth   18:1–11

There Christianity took up its pen and Paul wrote the first and oldest New Testament book, First Thessalonians.

Proconsul Gallio saves Paul from hostile Jews; the missionaries return
to Antioch via Ephesus, Caesarea, Jerusalem   18:12–22

Section E: Paul's Third Missionary Journey (A.D. 52–56)

Antioch in Syria	Philippi	Troas
Galatia	Thessalonica	Miletus
Phrygia	Beroea	Tyre
Ephesus	Corinth	Caesarea
Troas	Philippi	Jerusalem

Paul works in Ephesus until silversmith Demetrius raises a riot against
him in Diana's temple   19:1–10, 21–41

Perhaps Luke is writing here. Relics of Diana's temple can be
seen in the British Museum—bases of pillars which Paul's gar-
ments may have touched. (For reading Ephesians see page 103.)

At Miletus Paul says farewell to Ephesian elders   20:17–38

Paul had left Ephesus and gone into Greece. At Corinth he
wrote the Romans epistle (see page 97). Now on the way to
Jerusalem with the offering he had been collecting, he asks the
elders of the Ephesian congregation to meet him at its nearby
seaport.

Paul and party reach Jerusalem amid dire warnings   21:1–16

Section F: Paul's arrest, Trial, and Voyage to Rome; the Gospel in Rome (A.D. 56–61)

Jerusalem	Crete	Rhegium
Caesarea	Fair Havens	Puteoli
Sidon	Phoenix	Forum of Appius
Cyprus	Malta	The Three Taverns
Myra	Syracuse	Rome

Paul makes a vow; Jews from Asia stir riot in the temple courts; Roman
soldiers arrest him; his defense fails   21:17–22:24

The afternoon of Paul's life is at hand. Members of his own race
and religion considered him a deserter and enemy of their faith.

The prisoner is taken to Caesarea to save him from a plot on his life,
discovered and reported by his nephew   23:12–35

Paul, examined by Festus, appeals for trial by Caesar   25:1–12

Paul, shipwrecked on way to Rome, is saved by Maltese   27:1–28:16
The apostle arrives in Rome; teaches while under guard   28:17–31
He continues his mission with such helpers as Timothy, Mark,
and Luke. He also writes the "prison epistles": Ephesians, Philippians, Colossians, and Philemon, recommended for reading now.

Books of Epistle

The twenty-one New Testament epistles are our supreme biblical source, after the Gospels, (a) for theology—both dogmatics
and ethics—and (b) for churchmanship.

They should be recognized as letters about actual Christian
faith-living at their time of writing and, more importantly, having that same value now. There has been an unfortunate ten-
dency to treat them chiefly as foundational texts for more or less
difficult beliefs. Actually, being letters, they were "occasional"
documents, meaning there were specific reasons for their writing.
The authors were dealing directly with immediate, practical
needs of Christian persons and congregations. They meant to
help comrades in the faith-life to be sound in belief and exem-
plary in conduct. This would enhance the abundance of the
recipients' own lives and enable them to work more effectively
for Christ by witness of life as well as of lip. The authors wished
also to help those early church groups to grow in numbers and
influence while contributing toward community uprightness and
welfare.

While there are differing opinions concerning the circulation
of these epistles, they were probably written in somewhat the
following order, with likely dates:

Thessalonian letters (50)	Colossians, Ephesians, Philemon, Philippians (59–61)
Galatians (52)	Hebrews (90–95)
Corinthian letters (53–55)	James, John, First Peter (90–100)
Romans (55)	Jude, Timothy, Titus, Second Peter (after 100?)

This group of books includes short ones such as Philemon and
the epistles of John. As with minor prophets, brevity does not

equal uselessness. These short books, too, are rich with teaching values.

The Epistles can be divided into three basic classifications:

    I. *Pauline Epistles:* the letters of the apostle Paul—Romans through Philemon—with a theological emphasis. In limited space it must suffice to accept the traditional number of thirteen with "prison" epistles and "pastoral" ones.

    II. *Loyalty literature:* Hebrews, formerly ascribed to Paul, here considered a first instance of loyalty literature; others are "general epistles" and The Revelation.

    III. *General Epistles:* seven books, James through Jude, emphasizing churchmanship.

I. The Pauline Epistles. Paul has been called "a pastor by letter." While he went about, starting and directing the congregations he founded, he corresponded with persons and groups in order to lend a helping hand. Some letters were kept, copied, recopied, and later printed until now we can use what he taught in them.

Thirteen New Testament books have been credited to Paul's authorship though modern scholars hold that probably a few were not really completed by him. For our purpose it will be said that the thirteen include the oldest New Testament documents and were written while Paul was making his famous tours or was a prisoner in Rome. Some contradictory views will be considered later in introductions to doubtful books.

Paul had gone far afield in the continuing ministry of Christ. He would go to a town and, being himself a Jew by birth, teach first in a synagogue, hoping to win his racial brethren for Christianity. As a reader of The Acts knows, he would often be driven out of town by a mob turned hostile by his non-Jewish teaching. Usually, though, he had won converts enough to be the nucleus of a congregation to which he could return. Meantime, he would keep in contact with his beloved people by correspondence. Usually the letters were prompted by news of upsetting disturbances in a church, troublesome conditions in a community, or serious problems of individual members. As cause for our interest and gratitude, the problems were similar to those we moderns face.

How did Paul do his writing? Probably he would call a public letter-writer or a friend to take dictation. We have the name of one, Tertius, mentioned in Rom. 16:22. The scribe would bring a reed pen, a bottle of brownish ink, and some sheets of papyrus paper. Then the apostle would dictate, possibly writing a bit with his own hand to prove the letter was genuinely from him.

The emphasis in Paul's letters is on theology that includes ethics as well as doctrine. One's religion is one's living experience in the God-human relationship; theology deals with certain findings about belief and behavior within that experience. Such findings are the raw data from which to hold and speak or write a more or less systematic formulation that is one's personal theology with its two branches of dogmatics and ethics. Each Christian is to have his personal theology. Importantly, just as one's theology is fully learned only in living, the learning is to be lived. The dogmatics and ethics drawn from Paul's letters are to live again in one's thought, word, and deed.

ROMANS

He who through faith is righteous shall live. (1:17)

One day, probably in A.D. 55, Paul and his "secretary" sat down together in Corinth while the apostle dictated a letter to Christians who had formed a congregation in Rome. He yearned to visit that hub of world affairs in order to establish its important church more firmly. But he must first go to Jerusalem and deliver an offering he was gathering from his mission congregations for needy Christians in the Holy City.

Romans was not the first of Paul's epistles but likely the sixth. Yet it is easy to see why churchmen who formed the New Testament gave this one first place among the Epistles; it is the major teaching on the meaning of Christian faith-life.

We are saved by grace through faith in Jesus Christ. This is Paul's theme. In the King James Version it is, briefly: *The just shall live by faith* (1:17); the Revised Standard Version, Common Bible, has it: *He who through faith is righteous shall live.*

What is salvation? How are we saved? From what are we saved and to what are we saved? Paul is saying that Christian disciples and apostles are living a new life "in Christ." They are in new relationships with God, their inner selves, and their neighbors. They have not ceased to be sinners but they are justified, reconciled and redeemed sinners, no longer condemned. Further, they are subject to continuing renewal of spirit, with growth toward saintliness. Paul urges the Romans to accept God's proffered gift.

There will be fruits, both incoming and outgoing. The inward fruits will be such as love, peace, hope, and joy. Outgoing gifts are listed in Chapters 12 through 15, said to be the greatest passage on Christian behavior except the Sermon on the Mount.

It is interesting to reflect that Rome is now the center for one great branch of Christianity and that Paul's remains, as some say, rest outside Rome's ancient walls.

SELECTED READINGS

The apostle introduces himself and greets Roman Christians   1:1–15
See Paul's characteristic ways of opening and closing his letters.

Paul's gospel is about God's gifts to persons with faith   1:16,17
Theologically, persons are justified by grace through faith, appropriating God's gracious acceptance of the believer.

God has given a new standing to all believers   3:21–31
Paul is beginning to deal with the many fruits of faith.

". . . the free gift of God is eternal life in Christ . . ."   6:1–23
Believers may consider themselves (6:11) *dead to sin and alive to God in Christ Jesus.*

Believers are God's children, "fellow heirs" with Christ   8:12–17
". . . God works for good with those who love him . . ."   8:18–30
Nothing can separate believers from the love of God   8:31–39
Paul praises the "depth of the riches . . . of God . . ."   11:33–36

Be a "living sacrifice"   12:1–21
Never flag in zeal, be aglow with the spirit, serve the Lord.

Be an obedient citizen   13:1–7
Paul does not overlook public duties despite the state's enmity.

Be a Christian brother   14:10–15:7
Paul announces plans to visit the congregation   15:14–33
He will arrive—as a prisoner to be martyred.

Greetings to many friends and a benediction   16:1–27
In such conclusions to his letters we sense the warmth of Paul's
spirit and his zeal for his mission.

FIRST CORINTHIANS and SECOND CORINTHIANS

*So faith, hope, love abide . . . the greatest of these is love.
(2 Cor. 13:13)*

During the years A.D. 53–55 Paul is writing to the Christians
in Corinth, Korinthos on the map of Southern Greece. In ruins
uncovered there you can see stones from the small *tribunal* of
Gallio, proconsul who dispersed hostile Jews attacking Paul (Acts
18:12–17).

Paul had worked in Corinth for more than a year while on his
second missionary journey (Acts 18:1–11). Now on a third journey, he is writing the Corinthians from Ephesus in Asia Minor,
200 miles across the Aegean Sea (Acts, Chapter 19).

Biblical scholars say that really four letters have been combined in the biblical two. (It will be interesting to read them in
the order described here.) In 2 Cor. 6:14–7:1 we apparently
have only a fragment of the first. Paul seems to have written
about the immorality and unbelief of members that infected the
membership after he had left.

The Corinthians, replying to that first word from Paul, asked
a number of questions about problems in their troubled church.
As one example, what should they do about divisions among
their members? The apostle replied in what we call First Corin-

thians with its candid advice. Most important for us, he includes those choice chapters, the thirteenth on love and the fifteenth on resurrection. Paul attempted further to help the Corinthians by sending two of his "assistant pastors," Timothy and Erastus to them. These seem to have found that the Corinthians had turned against the apostle and even questioned his right to be called an apostle.

So Paul wrote a third letter, doubtless as painful to him as it was to them; 2 Cor. 10:1–13:14 is considered a part of it. Paul, being very human, indulges in a little boasting about his spiritual experiences and his perils in the service of Christ (11:16–12:13). Actually the Corinthians should have been commending him but he has to reproach them for deserting him.

Titus delivers this third letter and Paul waits anxiously for a reply. He even starts on his way to visit the erring congregation while hoping daily to meet Titus returning with good news. At length Titus comes and the news is good. Now the Corinthians welcome Paul's leadership.

Then the apostle could write the fourth letter, our 2 Cor. 1:1–9:15, full of gratitude and affection. Paul rejoices in their new attitude, forgives the Corinthians for their unkindness to him, and urges them to put their trust in the risen Christ.

SELECTED READINGS

First Corinthians

Paul preaches "Christ crucified," power and wisdom of God   1:18–31
This is reputed to be Paul's second, advisory letter.

There are divisions in the Corinthian congregation   3:1–15
Some members give allegiance to Paul, others Apollos or Cephas.

". . . you are God's temple . . ."   3:16,17;6:19,20
Bodies are to serve God's purposes.

"This is how one should regard us . . ."; an apostle's work   4:1–21
Paul looks at marriage   7:1–16;25–40
Help others live uprightly   8:1–13;10:14–33

Should they eat meat which, before they bought it at the market, had been used for animal sacrifice to idols? They should restrain themselves when others would be offended.

Win the contest through self-discipline 9:24–27
The stadium in which the Isthmian games were held for many years was located only a few miles from Corinth.

Participate reverently in the Lord's Supper 11:23–28
The Corinthians had not observed proper decorum at the communion table. This is the first written account of that Last Supper.

Among gifts in "the body of Christ," have one spirit 12:1-31
Among things that abide, love is the greatest 13:1-13
Addressing the quarreling Corinthians Paul had written in the preceding verse: *"And I will show you a still more excellent way."* This has been called Paul's "noblest utterance."

Know that as Christ arose, believers, too, will be raised; there is victory over death 15:1–58
Is this, instead of the thirteenth, Paul's greatest chapter?

"On the first day of every week . . ." 16:1–4
Paul is gathering the offering for needy believers in Jerusalem (Acts 24:17, Rom. 15:25, and 2 Cor. 9).

Second Corinthians

Paul gives thanks to the "God of all comfort" 1:1–11
Chapters 1 through 9 (except 6:14–7:1) are probably Paul's fourth and thankful letter. The Corinthians accept him now and (1:8) he has recovered from an *affliction* in which he *despaired of life itself.*

Paul, looking forward to the "house not made with hands" and being of "good courage," does not "lose heart" 4:1–5:10
Make "holiness perfect" 6:14–7:1
The fragment of Paul's first and otherwise lost letter.

Be an example to others in giving for the needy 8:1–9:5

Paul declares he is truly an apostle   10:1–11:11

In Paul's third and stern letter he must convince the Corinthians
he is worthy to be their leader in the work of Jesus Christ.

**Paul allows himself to boast of dangers he faced though he calls it "a
little foolishness . . ."**   11:16–12:13

Yet, as he says (12:10) *when I am weak, then I am strong.*

GALATIANS

For freedom Christ has set us free . . . (5:10)

In A.D. 52 Paul is on furlough in Syrian Antioch after a second
missionary journey. There he hears that opponents have been
working among his Christian converts in Iconium, Lystra, and
elsewhere. They have taught that Gentile converts must *live like
Jews* (2:14), especially honoring circumcision as a mark of Jew-
ishness. In this great charter of Christian liberty Paul opens the
church door wide for any believer to enter. Christianity must
forever be a world religion above race, nation, or former religious belief.

Yet Christian liberty means more. Believers have personal
freedom for abundant living—the rich, full, lasting, and victorious
living in Jesus Christ that John called eternal life. Christianity is
especially freedom from the legalism seen in the Pharisees who
painfully observed exact details for proper eating, washing,
working, and worshipping, meanwhile neglecting higher levels
of human and divine relationships. A Christian would be moved
by devotion instead of fear, rising above the goodness that is
obedience to law in creatively serving law's purpose.

Yet Paul wanted his people to observe two restrictions within
their freedom: (a) remember that salvation is a gift from God,
not the result of attaining merit in either law or liberty; (b)
know that Christian liberty gives no one the right to do nothing
at all or act just as he blithely pleases. A Christian will accept a
necessary measure of external discipline but aim to live by self-
discipline—built-in loyalty to Christ's advising, appealing, plead-

ing, warning. A person who abuses his liberty by lax living just naturally loses his freedom.

SELECTED READINGS

It was perhaps forty years before Luke wrote his account of it.

First here, in Paul's third epistle, he teaches his precious doctrine of justification by grace through faith. In Romans, his sixth epistle, he restates and elaborates it.

Not keeping the law but abiding in the relation of faith in Jesus Christ is the way of life with God.

So pertinent for this last quarter of the twentieth century!

Verses 22 and 23, listing the many fruits of the spirit are justifiably among the Bible's famous passages.

EPHESIANS

For he is our peace, who has . . . broken down the dividing wall of hostility . . . (2:14)

This letter of the first century could have been written for the late twentieth. East and West have been engaged in a colossal tug-of-war. There is establishment versus anti-establishment; there are even counter-counter-cultures. Persons are torn by inward tensions; many a family is a house divided against itself. The churches are only tardily tearing down their "iron curtains."

This shining signpost pointing the way toward unity, reads as if it had arrived in the morning mail!

There are differing opinions about the origin of Ephesians. To be cautious, Paul may have written it in his Roman prison about A.D. 59–61. It was perhaps a circular letter of which one copy went to the church in Ephesus and was preserved there.

Unity within ourselves will begin to exist as Paul writes here, when Jesus Christ becomes (2:14) *our peace.*

Unity in families will be attained when husbands, wives, and children (5:2) *walk in love as Christ loved us. . . .*

Unity among the churches requires building with Christ as cornerstone on a foundation of prophets and apostles (4:4) *one body and one spirit . . . one Lord, one faith, one baptism.*

Unity among the nations will arise when enough individuals possess the God-given (4:13) *knowledge of the Son of God.*

SELECTED READINGS

Paul gives thanks for blessings through Christ as sons and heirs and prays that Ephesians may enjoy them   1:1–23
Glorious unity flows from God's gift, new life in Christ   3:14–21
". . . maintain the unity of the Spirit in the bond of peace."   4:1–16

How often *one* and *unity*, also *all* and *every* appear!

Live on the positive side, be kind to one another . . .   4:25–32
Have Christly relationships as husbands, wives, children, parent, workers, employers   5:21–6:9
"Put on the whole armor of God . . ."   6:10–20

Bible readers like to think that Paul was looking at the equipment of his Roman soldier guard as he wrote.

PHILIPPIANS

" . . . *whatever is true . . . honorable . . . just . . . pure . . . lovely . . . gracious . . .*" (4:8)

This, there can be little doubt, is a "prison epistle" written when Paul was about to be martyred. People have called it his "last will and testament." Yet *joy* and *rejoice* appear in its verses more than a dozen times.

Paul is writing to "First Church" in Europe. Here Lydia had befriended the missionaries and Paul and Silas were freed from the jail by an earthquake. Probably now the Philippians were paying the rent on the rooms in which Paul was living and directing his mission while under house arrest.

The letter introduces one of the most interesting New Testament characters, Epaphroditus. When Paul was taken to Rome the Philippians heard about it. So they gathered a sum of money and sent it with Epaphroditus to help the apostle in any way possible. However, Epaphroditus became gravely ill. Paul knew that word would reach his family and worry them. So when Epaphroditus was well enough Paul sent him home with this letter. It would relieve the worry and prevent any possible criticism of Epaphroditus but also express Paul's thanks to the loyal friends who had made him glad by their steadfast and fruitful faith.

What is a worthy church like? Notice the Philippian congregation. Who is a noble Christian? See Paul with his ripe wisdom, deep humility, complete dedication, unfailing love, hope, joy, and confidence. Too, his spirit is at peace as, more than willing to die, he chooses to live for the sake of his beloved Philippian children in the faith.

SELECTED READINGS

"For to me to live is Christ and to die is gain."   1:19–30
"Have this mind among yourselves . . ."   2:1–11
Source of doctrine about Christ's "humiliation and exaltation."

Paul will send Timothy with Epaphroditus to Philippi   2:19–30
"I press on toward the goal . . ."   3:1–16
Inviting Philippians to share the goal of Christian maturity.

Paul bids Philippians rejoice and have God's peace   4:4-9
Verse 8 is another Pauline gem: *Finally . . . whatever is true. . . .*

Paul thanks his dear friends for their help though he has learned to be content in any condition 4:10-20

Another passage not to be missed!

COLOSSIANS

And let the peace of Christ rule in your hearts . . . (3:15a)

This is said to be another letter Paul wrote while a prisoner in Rome (59–61). His two years there did serve, as he said (Phil. 1:12), to *advance the gospel.* The city of Colossae was located more than a thousand miles from Rome. Yet from its congregation, Epaphras, who had founded the church, appeared at Paul's residence. He could make a good report on his members except false teachers were gaining ground among them. The heresy was doctrine of God, man, and salvation that cast a shadow over the primacy of Christ.

This was the sort of error to stir Paul most deeply. The letter's main purpose was to declare with all his force the sufficiency of Christ to meet man's most grievous needs. He exalts Christ as the All in All. He opens every stop of the organ to say (1:15) *He is the image of the invisible God . . .* and (2:13) *you, . . . dead in trespasses . . . God made alive together with him. . . .*

SELECTED READINGS

Paul praises the Colossians and prays for their fulness of life in Christ 1:3–14

Paul exalts Christ's person and work 1:15–23

Do not be deluded by human teaching; continue in Christ in whom ". . . the whole fulness of deity dwells bodily . . ." 2:1–23

Live the new life that is "hid with Christ in God." 3:1–17

Again Paul sees the mutual relations of God, self, and others.

Paul leaves admonitions about Christian family life 3:18–4:6

One of the best known passages on the subject.

FIRST THESSALONIANS and SECOND THESSALONIANS

Rejoice always, pray constantly, give thanks . . . (1 Thess. 5:16–18)

About the year A.D. 50 in Corinth, Paul called his scribe to take dictation. When he finished, the first Pauline epistle as well as the first New Testament book had been written.

Paul's second stop in Europe on his second missionary journey had been at Thessalonica, now Saloniki in eastern Greece. The apostle had been well received there but after only three sabbaths of teaching, Jewish enemies forced him to leave hastily in order to save himself and his companions from being mobbed. Naturally, as he travelled on he was anxious about the children in the faith whom he left behind. So he sent back Timothy, his assistant at the time, to see how things were going. Then, first at Athens and later at Corinth, he waited for news.

When Timothy came to Paul he could report that the Thessalonians were continuing in their new faith despite everything their enemies were doing. So Paul wrote our First Thessalonians to tell them how grateful and hopeful their courage and loyalty made him. Too, as Paul usually does, he offers the Thessalonians an abundance of advice about living wholesomely.

Further, as readers of Paul's epistles expect, he deals with a doctrinal problem. The Thessalonians had been grieving about the fate of those who had *fallen asleep* and, they feared, could not meet the Lord on his return. Paul assures them that the dead as well as the living will share in the Lord's victory. Meantime, since no one can know the time, the best preparation is to be soberly watchful.

Before many weeks, though, Paul had to write our Second Thessalonians largely about the same matter. Certain persons were thinking the second coming would occur so soon that they might as well stop working. Then, of course, in their idleness they would become a scandal to the church. Paul had already urged them to be industrious, setting before them his own example of supporting himself by his own hands, presumably weaving tentcloth. Now he gives them the verse Captain John Smith is said to have quoted to the members of the Jamestown community (2 Thess. 3:10): *If anyone will not work, let him not eat.*

SELECTED READINGS

First Thessalonians

The Thessalonians had welcomed Paul and his gospel	1:1–10
Paul is happy because the people are standing fast in the faith and life so recently entered	3:1–13
" . . . abstain from unchastity . . . work with your hands."	4:1–12
Await Christ with comfort and hope soberly, watchful	4:13–5:11

Those who die before the second coming will meet the Lord.

". . . hold fast what is good, abstain from . . . evil."	5:12–21

Second Thessalonians

The Thessalonians are doing well	1:3–12
Do not be deceived about Christ's second coming	2:1–12

The day of the Lord has not yet come.

"Brethren, do not be weary in well doing."	3:6–13

FIRST TIMOTHY, SECOND TIMOTHY, and TITUS

. . . that the man of God may be complete . . . (2 Tim. 3:16b)

These three epistles are called "pastoral" because they were addressed to pastors and deal with the work of pastors; yet there is abundant teaching in them for lay persons, too. Opinions differ about their origin. According to one view the books came from Paul on a fourth missionary journey. Some think he was released at his first trial in Rome, took this fourth journey, then was arrested a second time and sentenced to death. He had visited Ephesus, they say, and left Timothy in charge there. Then he went on to Macedonia (Greece) where he wrote First Timothy.

Next he visited the Mediterranean island of Crete and planted the church there. Leaving Titus as pastor to the Cretans, he returned to Corinth once more. There he wrote his letter to Titus. After arrest again and return to Rome for trial he wrote Second Timothy from his prison.

According to The Acts, though, we judge that Paul met his death after the first trial. There is also internal evidence that the pastorals may have been written much later, possibly at the end of the first century or even later. The authors, in that case, wrote "as if" Paul. By giving the sainted hero's name to the letters and addressing them to such prominent leaders as Timothy and Titus they would honor Paul, Timothy, and Titus. Also the work would get more attention.

It has been said that they are rightly called "Pauline epistles" because they contain important bits of real Pauline writing, possibly taken from notes sent by Paul to various persons or churches; 2 Tim. 4:6–22, in which the aging apostle seems to be saying farewell and so touchingly asks Timothy to bring the *cloak* and the *book*, may be such a passage. It includes the triumphant declaration any aging soul could wish to be able to make (4:7, 8): *I have fought the good fight . . . kept the faith. Henceforth there is laid up for me the crown of righteousness.*

SELECTED READINGS

First Timothy

Curb false teaching; salvation is in Christ	1:3–17
Pray for all men	2:1–7
Standards for church leadership	3:1–4:16

Who is a good leader in the church? A good follower? The questions are answered here and elsewhere in these epistles.

Instruction to a "man of God"; advice to the rich	6:6–16

Second Timothy

"Share in suffering . . ."	2:3–13
" . . . continue in what you have learned . . . believed . . ."	3:14–18
A glorious swan song by Paul	4:6–22

Titus

Instructions about church leadership   1:5–16
Since Cretans are always liars . . . (1:12) the church in Crete
needed Titus sorely to (1:5) *"amend what was defective."*

The pastor is to teach proper doctrine and behavior   2:1–15
Again, there is something for everyone.

PHILEMON

I appeal to you for my child, Onesimus. . . . (verse 10)

Somebody has said that this last Pauline epistle is "a window
into the heart of Paul." Written when he was a prisoner in Rome,
evangelizing as he suffered what in Hamlet is called "the law's
delay," it was a plea for the restoration of a runaway slave.

Philemon, to whom the letter is addressed, was a member of
the Colossian congregation. His slave, Onesimus (the name
means useful) had run away to Rome. A hunted criminal, he
had come to Paul's house and the apostle had won him for the
Christian way. If Onesimus returned to his master he could be
beaten, imprisoned, or put to death. So Paul asks Philemon to
take him back *no longer as a slave but . . . as a beloved brother.*

Since Tychicus is carrying Paul's letter to the Colossian congregation he and Onesimus travel together to Colossae. A religious film shows the two on their way, Onesimus carefully
guarding the treasured scroll that will win him his freedom.

Church history says that there was a bishop Onesimus. Was it
this man, set free by Philemon and entrusted with this high
position in the church? There can be blessed results when
Christians treat others as brothers.

SELECTED READINGS

Reading Philemon in its entirety will be choice moments with
the winsome spirit of Paul.

II. The Loyalty Literature. The epistle to the Hebrews holds its
position in our Bibles because it was once, though no more,

thought to have come from Paul. It does provide a fitting bridge between the Pauline epistles and the others—as the last of the books with the theological emphasis before those with a church-manship emphasis. Too, Hebrews stands at the head of what can be called loyalty literature. In a general way, Hebrews, the general epistles and The Revelation all are saying, "stand up, stand up for Jesus."

The half-century after Paul was a time of fearful testing for the new people of God. Beginning about the time of Paul's death the church suffered three bitter trials. Two were persecutions—by the Emperor Nero about A.D. 64 and in Domitian's reign A.D. 81–96. Nero, it has been said, perhaps wrongly, blamed Christians for setting fire to Rome although he did it himself. Domitian's government was trying to force everyone to worship Caesar, but Christians could not do this. So officers would arrest and drag them away to prison, perhaps to death. Possibly some of the bones we see in the catacombs may be the remains of Christians for whose loyalty our New Testament books were pleading.

The fall of Jerusalem was a third tragic event. Rome had ruled the city since 63 B.C., but the Jews opposed that rule. About A.D. 66 they began to revolt. Titus came with his legions to restore Roman control. Jerusalem was overthrown, A.D. 70, after a horrible siege. Then members and leaders of Christian congregations were killed or driven elsewhere in the empire.

It was natural that literature with loyalty as its keynote would develop. While writers were helping their readers to solve practical concerns of churches and persons, they would also plead for steadfastness in belief and in life that would honor, not dishonor, the Lord.

HEBREWS

Now faith is the . . . conviction of things not seen. (11:1)

Christianity has always been costly in human life—most of all, it may be hard to believe, in this twentieth century. Yet in Christianity's first generation Stephen, James, Peter, and Paul became martyrs. In the next half century there were likely tens of thousands of martyrs, especially in those persecutions under Nero and Domitian. At such times some Christians would crumple. So Hebrews along with the other loyalty books were meant to nerve Christ's followers for bearing their crosses.

The King James Version uses as the title for this book, "The Epistle of Paul the Apostle to the Hebrews," but scholars hold that its form is not like Paul's epistles and its language and teaching not identical with his. Who, then, was the author? Likely a member of the church in Rome, away from home, and writing to his brethren back in the city.

The time seems to be after one persecution, probably Nero's, and then during another, Domitian's. The Roman Christians are not prepared for this. Instead of lending Christianity in the whole empire the leadership which could be expected out of the great capital they could have let it perish at home.

The congregation had grown weary of well-doing. Its members had been only evangelized; they had not grown in Christ. The author tells them candidly that their educational program has been neglected (6:1–12). So their faith is shallow; their attitude apathetic, their service negligible. In Christ they have the greatest religion of all; they ought to be stalwart witnesses for it instead of succumbing under fiery trial.

The great chapter is the eleventh which begins with the notable definition of faith. Then it calls a long roll of heroes who bore trial triumphantly. Through faith, the writer declares, they (11:32–38) *conquered kingdoms, enforced justice . . . were tortured . . . were stoned . . . sawn in two; went about in skins of sheep and goats destitute, afflicted, ill-treated.* He closes with his mighty appeal for all Christians always (12:1): *Therefore, since we are surrounded by so great a cloud of witnesses, let us . . . run with perseverance the race that is set before us.*

SELECTED READINGS

God's self-revelation is consummated in the Son   1:1–4

Later verses and chapters show that Christ is superior to angels, Moses, and all preceding priests. Romans, remain loyal to him!

Be growing in Christianity   **5:11–6:8**
Hold fast with hope, confidence, endurance   **10:19–25;32–39**
During Nero's persecution the Romans had stood firm.

Faith's definition; be another hero of faith   **11:1–12:2**
Another of the Bible's great chapters. By faith, what one hopes for seems so near and things of the unseen world appear so real that a Christian acts as if they were present and visible.

Accept discipline as helpful   **12:3–11**
Words to be engraved deeply in memory!

"Let brotherly love continue."   **13:1–18**
The author speaks for love, contentment, doing good, helpfulness, hospitality, joy, obedience, praise, sharing, and worship.

III. The General Epistles. The next seven New Testament books are called "general epistles" but sometimes "catholic epistles," meaning "universal." Paul's epistles were usually addressed to a definite congregation or person; most of these were not. Their dates, as estimated by one scholar or another, cover nearly a century, A.D. 50–150, some in the third generation of Christianity.

There is no book of history, like The Acts for an earlier period, to tell the story of this one. Yet we do have these remaining books to provide a few suggestions. Too, they were loyalty literature, along with Hebrews and The Revelation; further, they stressed an honorable manner of community, domestic, and personal living. Yet there was a more specialized purpose for this writing. As Paul's epistles emphasize theology, these emphasize churchmanship. They can be seen as manuals for the activities of effective church management and membership.

The life of the young church would have been difficult enough without the disasters that befell it. There was a need for correct statements of truth about Jesus which the members would hold and ask their converts to believe. Too, that truth had to be kept pure from the teachings of those who misunderstood the faith or would have misused it. Besides, how was the church to be governed? How was its work in the world to be done? How were its membership rolls to be expanded? What forms of worship would be used? How would leaders be chosen, trained, and supported? How would members, both young and old, be educated?

These seven books of James through Jude, originally meant to help solve such problems in that early church, can serve similar purposes in current church life while they also have rich teaching values for church members' daily lives. James alone provides, among its half a hundred imperatives, something for just about any problem imaginable. First and Second Peter are not so fertile yet are unexpectedly germane. Epistles of John emphasize love as the ultimate motivation for all Christian activity. Jude pleads the necessity for sincereity versus hypocrisy in church matters; the passage on *fruitless tree* can rebuke many an indifferent individual on the church's membership rolls. All the books reprove heresy.

It could seem that the brevity of these books scarcely matches the magnitude of the church today. Yet their brevity can be an advantage. They are more simple, precise, direct, and easily comprehended than Paul's epistles or Hebrews. There is so much that needs no special effort at interpretation to sting, warn, guide, or inspire even a twenty-first century churchman.

JAMES

So faith by itself . . . is dead. (2:17)

It would seem unusual if the New Testament did not include one or more books made from parts of a sermon or a series of sermons. James is said to be such a book. There are wide differences in people's views about the book's author and date. Some have believed that it was written by the James who was a prominent leader in the young church in Jerusalem until he was martyred. If so, the book may have appeared as early as A.D. 45 and would be the earliest of all in the New Testament. Other persons notice that the author seems to have known the Sermon on the Mount, Paul's epistles, Hebrews, and First Peter; so he may have been some unknown James, writing about A.D. 100.

Regardless of any such matters, the book contains fifty-four important imperatives in its one hundred eight verses—as an instance (5:12): *let your yes be yes and your no be no. . . .* And here are a few of the preacher's themes:

Endure trial and temptation (Chapter 1).
Join works with faith (Chapter 2).
Control the tongue (Chapter 3).
Seek spiritual graces versus material treasures (Chapter 4).
Pray for the sick and evangelize the lost (Chapter 5).

SELECTED READINGS

"Count it all joy . . . when you meet various trials . . ."   1:1–5
Strengthened character may follow suffering.

Being doer of the word: the nature of true religion   1:22–27
" . . . show no partiality . . ."   2:1–13
". . . faith apart from works is dead."   2:14–26
True faith is dynamic love in action.

"And the tongue is a fire."   3:1–12
Could anyone write more fittingly about the "little member"?

"Do not speak evil against one another . . ."   4:11,12
"Your gold and silver have rusted . . ."   5:1–6
James has caution for the wealthy, encouragement for the poor.

The power of prayer   5:13–18

FIRST PETER and SECOND PETER

. . . we have been born anew to a living hope . . . (1 Pet. 1:3)

First Peter is a book for persecuted Christians. No one knows how many have pored over its pages during the hours before they were called to become martyrs. We can only guess how many are reading it now in lands where Christians lack religious freedom. It is perhaps easier for us North Americans and others to be Christians—at least by name—than not to be. While, then, we need not fear persecution we do live with other fears. This author bids all the fearful to look up and hope. The foundation for hope is quiet dependence on the Christ of peace in the inner spirit of a person who is active in love.

Scholars agree on the purpose of this book but not its date and authorship. One would think it was written by Simon Peter. Usually scholars say it reflects later times, perhaps A.D. 90–100 during Domitian's persecution. Then the author named it as if it were the sainted apostle's message to the persecuted.

Second Peter is not like First Peter. It is written in a different style, seemingly to a different group of people. While it is also loyalty literature its emphasis is on warning readers against false teachers especially concerning the second coming of the Lord. The author wants his readers to await that coming with assurance and patience, remembering that (3:8) *with the Lord one day is as a thousand years. . . .* As an unusual feature, he mentions Paul's epistles, saying that they are hard to understand (3:15, 16); he also reproduces almost all of Jude's second chapter with its invective against error. The major teaching value for us may be the warning against, for example, some of the wayward things we hear and see on the air waves.

The book is sometimes said to have been written near A.D. 150 making it the youngest of all biblical books.

SELECTED READINGS

First Peter

The author is thankful for living hope through Christ   1:3–25
It is also to be a challenge for holy living by the *born anew.*

A picture of the church as a spiritual house   2:4–10
"Honor all men. Love the brotherhood. Fear God."   2:11–17
Advice on Christians' civic relationships and family life-styles 2:18–3:7

FIRST, SECOND, and THIRD JOHN

*He who does not know love does not know God. . . . (1
John 4:8)*

These three books teach the supreme significance of love while
they also deal with the high themes of light and truth. Love is
mentioned more than 40 times, 20 times in the fourth chapter of
First John. Here, only here, we are told (4:8) that . . . *God is
love*; naturally the author sees the church as a fellowship in
bonds of love among God and men. The author also aims to
declare the whole truth about Jesus Christ as Son of God and
Son of Man. This was to oppose false teachers who either denied
that Jesus became a mortal man or did not accept him as God's
son. If anyone should ask, "What is God like?" John would
answer, "Look at Christ and see him."

Five New Testament books have "John" in their titles, suggesting that the author was "the beloved disciple." However, John
was a common name among early Christians as it is among us.
So students of the authorship of the books named John have
differing opinions. Here we shall say that the three epistles were
written by one author, scarcely the one who wrote the gospel,
maybe The Revelation. He seems to be writing in the beginning
of the second century to churches in the region of Ephesus.

First John was a circular letter carried to congregations by a
sort of circuit-riding missionary. Today copies would be dupli-
cated by machine and mailed to each congregation. The author
plunges headlong into a declaration of fellowship with the Father
and his Son, Jesus Christ—a thought repeated often. Soon, too,

he makes frequent references to sin and forgiveness. The love
theme enters after the short first chapter.

The false doctrine that denied the two persons of Christ is
introduced when John declares Jesus is the Son of the Father.
He treats the reverse error in 4:2: *every spirit which confesses
that Jesus Christ has come in the flesh is of God.* . . .

Second John seems like a short note to accompany the first
epistle to a certain church in error about Christ's nature. *Elect
lady* in its address means "church" and *the elder*, of course, is
John. In his greeting John proclaims Jesus Christ as *the Father's
Son.* . . . In verse 7 he speaks to those who, holding the other
error, will not acknowledge the coming of Jesus Christ in the
flesh. Yet, even before this, he pleads (verse 6b) *that you follow
love.*

Third John is one of the few personal letters. John asks a
friend, Gaius, to help on his way Demetrius who seems to be
carrying the correspondence. Gaius follows the truth and renders
service to the brethren, especially to strangers. In contrast Dio-
trephes opposes the elder. John hopes to visit the elect lady and
rebuke the troublesome brother.

SELECTED READINGS

First John

John writes of Christ, "the word of life . . ." and the Christian way
of fellowship with God and man   1:1–4
"God is light . . . walk in the light . . ."   1:5–2:11
"Do not love the world . . ."   2:15–17
"God is love . . ."; love one another in God's family   4:7–21
As John writes the good word: *perfect love casts out fear.*

Love God and his children, believe in the loving Son, overcome the
world, have eternal life   5:1–13

Second John and Third John

There is guidance for reading these books in their introductions
above.

JUDE

. . . contend for the faith . . . (1:3)

In this next to the last New Testament book an author sounds again the note that has been ringing throughout: believe in Jesus Christ steadfastly and live with becoming conduct. Yet Jude is chiefly an outburst against the sins of those who may be both wavering in their faith and living loosely. The author does not mince words as he condemns erroneous doctrine and its proponents whose teachings disturb congregations.

As one error, it seems that there was doubt abroad concerning the second coming of Christ and the judgment. Jude declares that the promise is sure. Further, the doctrine that persons may do whatever they please with their bodies if their spirits keep fellowship with God is false. Jude's readers are to be on their guard and do both: defend the true faith of the apostles and behave uprightly.

The book calls Jude a *brother of James.* However, it is said that this author condemns heresies which came later than a brother of the martyred James could have lived. Some hold that the date is possibly A.D. 125.

There is still use for the righteous indignation Jude displays when he calls the erring ones *waterless clouds* and *wild waves.* The book is cherished most for its beautiful concluding prayer: *Now to him who is able to keep you from falling . . . to the only God, our Saviour . . . be glory, majesty, dominion, and authority, before all time and now and for ever. Amen.*

SELECTED READINGS

The short book can profitably be read in its entirety.

Book of Apocalypse

The final message of the Bible is written as a mystifying form of literature called apocalypse, writing that professes to "reveal the ultimate divine purpose." Apocalypses appear in Ezekiel,

Daniel, and other prophets; "the little apocalypse" in Matt. 24 is an example from the teaching of Jesus. Frequently, apocalypse deals with "the day of the Lord" (Old Testament) or Judgment Day (New Testament).

Apocalypses characteristically refer backward to historical events and often use symbols out of older writings. However, the writers are even more conscious of their own times which were usually days of crisis, danger, and suffering. Thus, in the light of both history and current events, apocalyptists were seeking to unveil the hidden, render clear the mysterious, disclose the future. They did it chiefly by describing visions and, for safety's sake, usually wrote in a sort of code with cryptic language in which numbers, animals, and strange names stood for persons, places, and ideas. A plain-spoken book could have become evidence to condemn anyone who possessed a copy.

Literalistic interpreters have long used the lofty chapters of works like The Revelation for precise predictions about to be fulfilled on a date that wise decoders can reckon. As one instance, a white-clad group assembled on a hilltop near Toronto one morning in June of 1930 to await the end. But the newspapers had to record one more instance of misused biblical material which should be understood not so much as precise prediction of the future as basic teaching for all time.

Rightly used, The Revelation should nurture a great belief: Christ has come and will come. God is still working in creation, providence, judgment, redemption, and sanctification. His people are participating in a drama that is moving on with its God-given plot. Seed has been sown; the plant is growing; there will be a harvest. Christians are citizens in a kingdom that is in being while it is becoming what it shall be.

THE REVELATION TO JOHN

Blessed are the dead who die in the Lord henceforth. (14:13)

The Bible has taught already that God is, God acts, and God

loves as his children should. It ends with The Revelation's ringing declaration that God and his people will be victorious.

In the book's dreadful times during Domitian's persecution
near the end of the first century, the Roman empire was under
a pall of evil and fear. Who, more readily than the Christians,
could be blamed? They had refused to obey the emperor's edict
that he be called "lord and god." Christians could not worship
any man, least of all such a brutish one. Thousands were treated
as traitors, some imprisoned or exiled, others thrown to the wild
animals in the Colosseum.

The author himself is a victim. We can know him only as some
John, possibly a bishop of churches in what is southwestern
Turkey. Now a prisoner in a concentration camp on Patmos, an
island a hundred miles out in the Aegean Sea, he is writing to
threatened mainland congregations, striving to brace them to
endure.

His book opens simply with seven letters to seven churches
that it faults for weaknesses and praises for strengths. Then the
reader enters a world of fantasy somewhat like a sacred opera
with solos and choruses, accompanied by harps and trumpets,
while color and sound effects surpass anything on land or sea.
Seven visions are reported, some with seven parts.

We read the book best as an apocalypse of the fall of Rome
and the evil for which it stands. It is also a promise of ever-
recurring as well as final victory for Christ and his own. Does
God face defeat? No. Will the work of Christ fail in the end? No.
Will the teachings of biblical books prove to be deceptions? No,
the very opposite. God is just, righteous, and merciful—powerful,
too. So everything godly will live; while all else perishes Christ
and his church will triumph.

This can be a great book for days in which the world is over-
shadowed by the threat of nuclear extinction or planetary dete-
rioration through ecological mismanagement. *The kingdom of
the world has become the kingdom of our Lord and of his Christ,
and he shall reign forever and ever.* That verse (11:15), celebrated in Handel's *Messiah*, declares the victory of the Christian's Lord. And this is to be the victory of the Christian person

who remains loyal (2:10): *Be faithful unto death, and I will give you the crown of life.*

SELECTED READINGS

John is to write a book and send it to seven churches   1:9–20
The book opens with promises for the one *who conquers.*

John writes first to the Ephesian Church, busy but not loving   2:1–7
John writes last to Laodicea, lukewarm, wealthy but poverty-stricken
in its spiritual life.   3:14–22
Verse 20 gives us the picture of Christ knocking at the door.

John reports a first vision: the throne and the Lamb   4:1–5:14
The four horsemen of the apocalypse   6:1–8
Riders with horses white, red, black, and pale stand respectively
for conquest, war, famine, and death.

Blessed martyrs serve at the throne of God   7:13–17
Recall the circumstances of the threatened souls who first heard:
God will wipe away every tear. . . .

The doom of great Babylon (Rome)   18:11–24
"Hallelujah . . ."   19:1–6
The final judgment; the book of life described   20:11–15
John has a vision of a new kingdom's arrival   21:1–22:5
Interpreters think of the Bride as the people of the church and
the New Jerusalem as the future in which Christ as the loving
God is head of the family in the new home.

The Unity of the Bible

While there are two Testaments with 66 books, there is one
Bible. The book is so large and complex that we must ordinarily
consider it bit by bit, but this must not blind us to its totality.
The whole of the Bible is more than the sum of its parts.

The history of the total book—its origin, development, trans-
mission, distribution, and universal use—has more than a "hint

of eternity" about it. The wholeness of it bears the imprint of continuing life. It appears as truly Word of Life, word from God for God's life with man and man's life with God, self, and neighbor.

When we think of the two Testaments together we see clearly how Christ is the central figure in it all. The scriptural movement is forward toward him and onward with him. There is a revelation of his preeminence.

The Bible from first to last is an account of an age-long movement of faith and life which found its climax in Jesus Christ. The movement lives on in his church in which each member has a participant's challenging and satisfying role.

In the unity of it all we see that God has been revealing himself as one God, creative and provident, incarnate in Jesus Christ, and continuing his work in the Holy Spirit.

When persons see, through the Bible's totality, what God is able to do for his people and say to them for their needy lives through so long a span of time, he appears as truly a living God. Further, the whole Bible shows how no powers or principalities have been able to halt the purpose of that God in the midst of his people. Finally, throughout this Word of Life, God is love as seen especially in Jesus Christ.

It is in the kingdom of this one living, loving, and unconquerable God that the Bible helps Christians find themselves to be blessed citizens.

Afterword: Let the Word of Life Live

No one writes a serious book just for the sake of writing it and having people read it; he wants some good result to follow the reading. This principle of writing for worthy use pertains more fully to the Bible than any other book. It is the Book of which God is the great Author. He gave it through human life so that it can go back into life again. Further, every human writer wanted something to happen because he wrote what he did. So the Bible is a book of the unfinished task. Its authors could tell us how a kingdom had begun; they had to leave with us their hopes for its fulfillment. There are temples to build, with the Holy Spirit guiding human spirits and lending them the essential power.

It has been said that the Revised Standard Version of the Bible has been put in "living language." That is good, but the real issue is something else: Will the version become "lived language?" Its readers must translate it once more—into what the Bible calls living epistle.

Doubtless that result is what the revisers had in mind when they put these words at the conclusion of their preface: "It is our hope and our earnest prayer that this Revised Standard Version of the Bible may be used by God to speak to men in these momentous times, and to help them to understand and believe and obey His Word."

Interestingly enough, the King James translators had written similarly, "A blessed thing it is . . . when God speaketh unto us, to hearken; when he setteth his word before us, to read it; when he stretcheth out his hand and calleth, to answer, 'Here I am . . . to do thy will, O God'."

And both those expressions are strikingly like the quaint prayer of John Wycliffe in his preface to the first complete translation of the Bible into English which he made about 1400: "God grant us to ken and to kepe Holi Writ and to suffer joiefulli some pain for it at the last."

Now—as God wills, writers strove, and translators prayed—let the Word of Life live in and through all those who use this book to "the increase among men of the love of God and neighbor."

HUMAN CONCERNS
IN THE BIBLE

Human Concerns
in the Bible

Abide: John 15:4; 1 Cor. 13:13; 1 John 4:12-16
Abundant, abound: John 10:10; 1 Cor. 15:58; 2 Cor. 9:8; Phil. 4:12
Age: Ps. 37:25,26; Phil. 3:14,15; Titus 2:2,3; 1 Pet. 5:1-5
Anger: Prov. 16:32; Matt. 5:21-26; Eph. 4:26; James 1:19,20
Anxiety (*see* Worry)
Ask (and receive): Matt. 7:7-11; John 11:22; Phil. 4:6
Authority:
    Bible's: Matt. 7:24-29; 2 Tim. 3:16,17; 2 Pet. 1:20,21 (*see* Bible)
    Civil: (*see* Citizenship)
    God's: John 12:49; Acts 1:7; Rom. 13:1 (*see* God)
    Christ's: Matt. 7:29; Mark 12:24-33; John 14:10

Backsliding, return: Jer. 8:5; Matt. 26:69-75; Luke 9:62; Heb. 6:4-6
Beatitudes: Matt. 5:1-12
Believe, belief (*see* Doubt, Faith, God, Jesus Christ):
    General: Mark 9:23; 11:24; 1 Cor. 13:7
    In God: 2 Chron. 20:20; Mark 1:14,15; John 14:1
    In Jesus Christ: John 3:16; 11:25,26; Rom. 10:9-11
Benediction: Num. 6:24-26; 2 Cor. 13:14; Jude vs. 24,25
Benefits, blessings: Ps. 103:1-5; 1 Cor. 2:9; 2 Cor. 9:8
Bible, scripture: Jer. 36:1-32; John 20:31; Rom. 15:4; Heb. 1:1,2
Bless: Gen. 12:1-3; Num. 6:24-26; Ps. 103; Luke 6:28
Blessed: Job 1:21; Ps. 1:1-6; Matt. 5:1-12; James 1:12
Body:
    Christ's: (*see* Church, Communion, Jesus Christ)
    Man's: Matt. 6:25; 1 Cor. 6:19,20; 9:27; 2 Cor. 5:1-5
Brotherhood, brotherliness: Prov. 17:17; Matt. 5:21-24; Luke 15:11-39
Burden, care: Ps. 55:22; Matt. 11:28-31; Gal. 6:2; 1 Pet. 5:6,7

Call:
    Christ's, God's: Jer. 1:1-19; Mark 3:13-19; Eph. 4:1-3; Rev. 3:20
        (*see* Discipleship)
    Ours (upon Christ, God): Pss. 4:3; 141:1,2; Luke 6:46; 2 Tim.
        2:22 (*see* Witnessing)
Caring:
    God's for us: Ps. 23:1-6; Matt. 6:25-33; Luke 12:4-7
    Ours for others: Matt. 25:31-46; Luke 10:29-37; Gal. 6:2; 1 John
        3:17 (*see* Helping, Kindness)
Chastening: (*see* Discipline)
Children: (*see* Family)
Choice, choose: Deut. 30:19; Job 34:4; Luke 10:38-42; John 15:16
Christ: (*see* Jesus Christ)
Christmas: Isa. 9:2-7; Matt. 1:18-25; Luke 2:1-20

Church: Matt. 16:18; Acts 2:43-47; Rom. 12:4-7; Rev. 1:4-3:22 (*see* Body of Christ, Worship)

Citizenship: Matt. 22:17-21; Rom. 13:1-7; 1 Pet. 2:13-17

Cleansing: Ps. 51:1-12; Isa. 1:16,17; 2 Cor. 7:1; 1 John 1:5-9 (*see* Renewal, Turn)

Comfort: Isa. 40:1-11; Matt. 5:4; John 14:1-7; 2 Cor. 1:3-7; 2 Thess. 2:16,17

Comforter, counselor: (*see* Holy Spirit)

Commandments:

   Great: Matt. 22:34-39; Mark 12:28-34

   New: John 13:34; 1 John 2:7-11

   Ten: Exod. 20:1-17; Matt. 5:19-47; Rom. 13:8-10

Communion (holy), Eucharist: Matt. 26:26-29; 1 Cor. 11:23-33

Complaining, fretting, murmuring: Eph. 4:31,32; Phil. 2:14

Confession:

   Of Christ: Matt. 16:13-17; John 21:15-17; Phil. 2:9-11 (*see* Believe, Faith)

   Of sin: Pss. 32:5; 51:1-9; Luke 15:11-24; 1 John 1:8-10 (*see* Forgiveness, Repentance)

Contentment: Matt. 11:28-30; Phil. 4:11-13; 1 Tim. 6:6-8; Heb. 13:5 (*see* Complaining, Peace, Rest)

Conversion: Luke 15:11-24; Acts 10:44-48; 22:6-16; Eph. 2:12,13

Cooperation: (*see* Harmony, Unity)

Courage: Josh. 1:9; Ps. 27:1,14; 1 Cor. 16:13; Heb. 13:6

Covet: Exod. 20:17; Luke 12:15; Heb. 13:5

Crossbearing: Matt. 10:37-39; 16:24; Luke 14:27; James 1:1-2

Death: Ps. 23:4; Isa. 43:2; John 14:1-3; 1 Cor. 15:54-56; Rev. 21:3,4

Deeds: Jer. 7:3; Col. 3:17; Titus 3:14; 1 John 3:18 (*see* Doing, Works)

Discipleship: Matt. 18:1-4; Mark 3:13-19; Luke 14:25-33; John 13:1-11 (*see* Call, Witnessing)

Discipline, chastening: Job 5:17,18; Prov. 3:11,12; 1 Cor. 9:24-27; Heb. 12:1-11

Discouragement, depression, despair: Ps. 22:1-5; Lam. 3:31-33; Luke 18:1-8; Rom. 8:31-39 (*see* Comfort, Hope, Sorrow, Joy)

Doing: Matt. 7:21-27; Luke 10:38-42; Gal. 6:9,10; 1 Tim. 6:18-19; James 1:22-25 (*see* Deeds, Works)

Doubt, unbelief: Matt. 14:31; 21:21; Heb. 10:21,22; James 1:5-8 (*see* Believe, Faith, Trust)

Duty, responsibility: Eccles. 12:13; Mic. 6:8

Easter: Matt. 28:1-10; Mark 16:1-8; Luke 24:1-12; John 20:1-18

Enemy: Prov. 25:21; Matt. 5:43-47; Acts 7:60; Rom. 12:14-20 (*see* Love, Peace, War)

Endurance: Matt. 24:12,13; Rom. 5:3-5; 1 Cor. 10:13; 13:7; 2 Tim. 4:6-8 (*see* Faithfulness, Steadfastness)

Eternal Life: Matt. 19:16-22; 25:31-46; John 3:16; 11:25,26; 1 Tim. 6:12; 1 John 3:2 (*see* Immortality, Resurrection)

Evening: Gen. 1:5; Ps. 141:1,2; Eccles. 11:6
Evil: Ps. 34:1-18; Prov. 6:16-19; Rom. 1:28-32; 7:21-23

Faith: Hab. 2:4; Mark 4:35-40; Rom. 1:16,17; Heb. 11:1-12:3; James
    2:14-17 (*see* Believe, Trust, Works)
Faithfulness: Josh. 24:14,15; Ps. 101:1-6; Luke 16:10-13; Gal. 5:22,
    23 (*see* Endurance, Steadfastness)
Family:
    Children (sons, daughters, brothers, sisters): Exod. 20:12; Ps. 133:
        1-3; Eph. 6:1-3; 1 John 2:9,10
    Group: Prov. 17:6; Luke 15:11-32; John 19:25-27; 1 Cor. 13:1-13
    Parents (father, mother): Exod. 20:12; Deut. 6:6,7; Eph. 6:4 (*see*
        Brotherhood, Marriage, God)
Fault-Finding: (*see* Judging)
Fear: Pss. 23:1-6; 27:1-14; Mark 4:35-41; Luke 12:6,7; John 14:27;
    Heb. 13:6 (*see* Courage, Worry)
Fellowship:
    With God: Ps. 105:4; Acts 8:18-21; 10:20; 2 Cor. 6:14-18
    With Jesus Christ: John 15:14,15; 1 Cor. 1:9; 1 John 1:3
    With man: Ps. 133:1-3; Matt. 18:19,20; Acts 2:44-47; 1 John 1:1-3
        (*see* Brotherhood, Communion, God, Jesus Christ)
Fighting: 2 Cor. 7:5; Eph. 6:10-17; 1 Tim. 6:12; 2 Tim. 4:6-8
Find (see and; and lose): Prov. 21:21; Matt. 7:7,8; 10:39; Luke 15:
    3-7 (*see* Lost, Seeking)
Foolishness: Prov. 1:7; Matt. 7:26,27; 25:1-12; Luke 12:13-21
Forgiveness:
    Others: Mark 11:25; Luke 17:1-4; Acts 7:59; Eph. 4:32
    Personal: Ps. 130:1-8; Isa. 1:18-20; Matt. 6:9-15; Luke 7:36-50
        (*see* God, Jesus Christ, Repentance, Sin)
Free, freedom: John 8:31-36; Rom. 6:22; Gal. 5:1; 1 Pet. 2:16
Friendship, friends: 1 Sam. 20:12-17; Prov. 17:17; John 15:13-15
Giving, charity: Matt. 25:31-46; Luke 18:18-23; Acts 20:35; 2 Cor.
    8:1-7 (*see* Money, Offering, Sharing)

Golden Rule: Matt. 7:12
God (*see* Jesus Christ, Holy Spirit, Trinity)
    Almighty, omnipotent, strong: Job 38:1-41; 42:2; Luke 18:27
    Approachable, accessible: Deut. 4:29; Matt. 5:8; 11:28; Rom. 5:1
    Creator: Gen. 1:1; Job 33:4; 38:1-41; Ps. 104:1-35
    Eternal, everlasting: Deut. 33:27; Dan. 4:34; Rev. 4:8
    Faithful, steadfastly loving: Pss. 13:5,6; 136:1-26; Rom. 8:31-39
    Father (and children): Pss. 68:5; 103:13; Matt. 6:8-13
    Forgiving, reconciling, remitting: Matt. 6:9-15; Mark 2:6-12; Luke
        23:34; 1 John 1:9
    Good, kind: 1 Chron. 16:34; Zeph. 3:5; Acts 14:16,17; Rom. 2:4
    Helper, refuge: Ps. 46:1-11; Jer. 17:14; Matt. 7:24,25; Heb. 13:6
    Holy, righteous, just: Lev. 19:2; Ps. 99:9; Isa. 5:16; Rev. 4:8
    Judge: Ps. 82:8; Isa. 33:22; Matt. 25:31-46; John 8:16 (*see* Jesus
        Christ, Judgment Day, Last Things)

King, kingdom, dominion, reign, rule, realm: Ps. 24:7-10; Matt.
    6:9-13; 13:1-52; 1 Tim. 6:15
Loving: Mal. 1:2; John 3:16; 17:26; Rom. 8:31-39; 1 John 3:1
Merciful, compassionate: 2 Chron. 30:9; Isa. 49:13; Phil. 4:14
One, unity, trinity: Deut. 6:4; Eph. 4:4-6; Rev. 1:8
Present, near, omnipresent, in us, with us: Isa. 43:1,2; Matt. 28:20;
    John 14:23; Acts 17:27-29
Provident: Eccles. 5:19; Ps. 23:1-6; Matt. 10:29-31; 2 Cor. 9:8,9
Wise, omniscient: Isa. 40:13,14; Rom. 11:33,34; 1 Cor. 8:3
Working, works: Job 37:14; Ps. 92:5; John 5:17; Rom. 8:28
Good, goodness:
    Deeds: Matt. 19:16-22; Luke 6:27; Heb. 13:16; Gal. 6:10
    Life: Luke 10:38-42; Phil. 4:8; 1 Pet. 3:8-12; 4:7-11
    Person: Ps. 1:1-6; Mic. 6:6-8; Matt. 12:33-37
    Works: Gal. 5:19-23; Eph. 2:10; Rom. 12:1-21; James 2:20,26
Gospel: Mark 1:15; John 3:16,17; Rom. 1:16,17; 2 Tim. 1:8-14
Gossip, backbiting, slander: Exod. 20:16; Ps. 15:1-3; Rom. 1:28-32;
    1 Tim. 5:13 (*see* Witness, False)
Greatness: Matt. 5:19; 18:1-4; 20:20-28; Luke 9:48
Greed, avarice: Prov. 16:8; 1 Kings 21:1-19; Matt. 16:26 (*see* Covet)
Growth: Luke 2:46-52; Eph. 4:13-16; Heb. 5:11-6:8; 2 Pet. 3:18
    (*see* Knowledge, Learning)
Guidance: Pss. 73:24; 119:105; John 16:13; Rev. 7:17 (*see* Word)
Guilt: Exod. 20:7; Ps. 51:1-12; 1 John 1:8-10 (*see* Forgiveness, Sin)

Happy, happiness: Ps. 128:1-6; Prov. 3:13-18; Matt. 5:2-11 (*see* Joy)
Harmony: Gen. 13:8; Matt. 12:25; Col. 3:14 (*see* Cooperation, Unity)
Hate: Lev. 19:17,18; Matt. 5:43-45; 1 John 2:9-11 (*see* Forgive)
Health, healing: Ps. 116:1-7; Isa. 38:16; Luke 9:11; Acts 3:16 (*see*
    Sickness; Jesus Christ Healing)
Hearing, hear: Jer. 29:12,14; Matt. 7:24-27; James 1:22-25; Rev. 1:1-3
Heart: Ps. 51:10-12; Matt. 5:8; Luke 16:15; John 14:27
Heaven: Matt. 5:12; 6:9; 19-21; 2 Cor. 5:1-8; Rev. 21:1-4
Helping: Eccles. 11:1; Isa. 58:7; Matt. 25:31-46; Luke 10:29-37 (*see*
    Neighbor, Serve, Sharing)
Holiness, godliness: Lev. 11:44,45; Eph. 4:22-32; 1 Tim. 4:6-10; 1
    Pet. 1:13-16 (*see* Good, Righteousness)
Holy Spirit: John 16:7-13; Acts 1:8; 2:1-4; 1 Cor. 12:4-13
Honesty, deceit, falsehood, hypocrisy, lying: Job 27:1-5; Prov. 12:17-
    22; Matt. 23:13-29; John 18:15-27 (*see* Truth)
Hope, optimism: Lam. 3:22,24; Rom. 5:1-5; 1 Cor. 13:7,13
Humility: Mic. 6:6-8; Matt. 5:5; 18:2-4; Luke 18:9-14; John 13:1-11

Immortality: John 11:25,26; 1 Cor. 15:51-53; 2 Tim. 1:10; 1 John
    2:17 (*see* Eternal Life, Resurrection)
Impartiality: Matt. 5:45; Rom. 2:11; James 2:8,9

Jealousy: Song of Sol. 8:6; Rom. 13:13; 1 Cor. 13:4; James 3:14,16
Jesus Christ, life: (*see* God, Holy Spirit, Trinity)

Baptism: Matt. 3:13-17; Mark 1:9-11; Luke 3:21,22

Birth: Matt. 1:18-2:12; Luke 2:1-20

Death, crucifixion, burial: Matt. 27:32-66; Mark 15:21-47; Luke 23:23-56; John 19:17-42

Last Supper: Matt. 26:17-29; John 13:1-20

Last Week: Matt. 21:1-27:31; Mark 11:1-15:39; Luke 19:29-23: 49; John 12:12-19:20

Public Ministry:

    Healing (instances in miracle narrative): Matt. 8:1-33

    Preaching (example, Sermon on the Mount): Matt. 5:1-7:29

    Teaching (examples in parable): Matt. 13:1-51; Luke 15:1-32

Resurrection, appearances, ascension: Matt. 28:1-20; Mark 16:1-8; Luke 24:1-53; John 20:1-31

Temptation: Matt. 4:1-11; Mark 1:12,13; Luke 4:1-13

Jesus Christ, person:

    Divine (Son of God): Matt. 3:16,17; John 1:1-3; 17:1; Phil. 2:5-7

    Forgiving: Luke 23:34; Eph. 4:32; Col. 3:13,14

    Friendly: Luke 10:38-42; 19:2-9; John 15:14,15; Rev. 3.20

    Helpful, beneficent, compassionate: Matt. 4:23,24; Luke 13:34; Acts 10:38; 2 Cor. 8:9

    Holy, pure, sinless: Matt. 27:19; Heb. 4:15; 1 Pet. 1:18,19

    Human (Son of Man): Matt. 8:20; Luke 19:10; John 1:14; Phil. 2:5-8

    Humble, lowly, meek: Matt. 9:10-12; John 13:1-11; Phil. 2:8

    "I am": Bread of Life: John 6:35; Light of the World: John 8:12; Door of the Sheep: John 10:7; Good Shepherd: John 10:11; Resurrection and the Life: John 11:25; Way, Truth, Life: John 14:6; True Vine: John 15:1

    Loving: Luke 13:34; John 13:23; Rom. 8:35-39; Eph. 3:17-21

    Merciful, gentle, kind, patient: Matt. 14:25-32; 2 Cor. 10:1; James 5:11; Rev. 1:3-10

    Presence, communion, fellowship, indwelling, "with you": Matt. 28:20; John 14:23; Eph. 3:17; 2 Cor. 13:5

    Winsome, inviting, welcoming: Matt. 11:28; Luke 6:12-16; John 21:15-17

Jesus Christ, work:

    Atonement: John 1:29; 1 Cor. 5:7; 1 Pet. 1:18,19; Rev. 12:11

    Healing, preaching, teaching (see Public Ministry)

    King, kingdom, Lord: Matt. 3:2; Luke 11:2; Rom. 14:17; parables of the kingdom, Matt. 13:1-52

    Judgment: see Judgment Day, Last Things

    Mission: Luke 4:16-21; 19:10; John 6:38-40; 1 Tim. 1:15

    Salvation (Savior): Luke 2:11; Acts 5:31; 1 Tim. 1:15; 1 John 4:14

    Redemption (Redeemer): Rom. 1:16; 1 Cor. 1:30; Col. 1:14

    Second Coming: 1 Thess. 3:11-13,51; 2 Thess. 2:1,2; 2 Pet. 3:10

    Servant: John 13:1-17; Acts 3:13; Phil. 2:5-8

    Suffering: see Last Week, Death

Joy, gladness: Ps. 16:11; Luke 15:7; John 15:11; Acts 2:28

Judging, criticizing, fault-finding: Matt. 7:1-5; Rom. 2:1-3; 14:10-13;
    James 4:11-13
Judgment Day: Matt. 25:31-46; John 5:25-29; 1 Thess. 5:1-11; 2 Pet.
    3:10 (see Last Things)
Justification: Rom. 3:26; 5:1; Gal. 2:15,16; Titus 3:4-8
Justice, injustice: Amos 5:24; Mic. 6:6-8; Luke 11:42; Phil. 4:8

Kindness: Mic. 6:1-8; Matt. 5:38-42; 1 Cor. 13:4-7 (see Mercy)
Kingdom: Matt. 13:1-25 (parables of); Luke 17:20-37; 2 Pet. 1:10,
    11; Rev. 11:15 (see God, Jesus Christ)
Knowledge, wisdom: 2 Chron. 1:7-12; Prov. 8:10,11; Eccles. 9:13-16

Last Things: Matt. 25:31-46; 1 Pet. 1:3-9; Rev. 21:1-4 (see Judgment
    ment Day, Jesus Christ—Resurrection, Second Coming)
Law: Ex. 20:1-17; Matt. 5:17-20; Luke 10:25-28; Rom. 13:10; James
    1:22-25 (see Commandments, Obedience, Works)
Learning: Ps. 119:71-73; Matt. 11:29; Heb. 5:11-6:3; 2 Tim. 2:15
    (see Growth, Knowledge, Understanding)
Life: Matt. 16:25,26; John 14:6; Acts 17:28; Phil. 1.27-30 (see
    Abundant, Eternal Life, Renewal)
Live: Hab. 2:4; Luke 4:4; 10:25-28; John 11:25,26
Lonely, forsaken: Deut. 31:6; Matt. 18:19,20; Rom. 8:35-39
Lord's Prayer: Matt. 6:9-15
Lost: Ps. 119:176; Isa. 6:5; Matt. 18:10-14; Luke 15:1-32; John 18:9
    (see Redemption, Salvation)
Love:
    For God: Deut. 6:5; 10:12; Mark 12:28-34; Luke 11:42; Rom. 8:28
    For Jesus Christ: Matt. 22:37-39; John 8:42; 21:5-17; Eph. 3:19
    For Others: Lev. 19:17,18; Matt. 5:43-47; John 13:34,35; 1 Cor.
        13:1-13
    For Self: Lev. 19:18; Matt. 22:37-39; Luke 10:27

Man: Gen. 1:26-31; Ps. 8:1-9; Matt. 4:4; 12:12; 15:10,11 (see
    Woman)
Marriage, husband, wife: Prov. 31:10-31; Song of Sol. 8:6,7; Matt.
    19:3-9; Col. 3:18,19; 1 Pet. 3:1-7 (see Family)
Mercy: Mic. 6:8; Matt. 5:7; 18:23-35; Luke 10:29-37 (see Pity)
Money: Eccles. 2:1-11; Luke 12:13-21; Heb. 13:5; 1 Tim. 6:17-19
    (see Giving, Greed, Treasures, Wealth)
Morning, dawn, awake: Job 38:7; Pss. 88:13; 119:148; Eccles. 11:7

Need, poverty, want: Ps. 72:1-14; Phil. 4:10-13,19; 1 John 3:17 (see
    Giving, Helping, Sharing)
Neighbor: Exod. 20:12-17; Prov. 27:10; Matt. 22:34-39; Luke 10:29-
    37
Night: Pss. 4:8; 63:5-8; Prov. 3:21-24; Luke 6:12; Rev. 22:1-5
New Year: Pss. 65:9-11; 102:25-28; Hab. 3:2; Heb. 1:10-12; Phil. 3:
    12-16 (see Praise, Prayer, Providence, Thanksgiving)

Obedience, disobedience: 1 Sam. 15:22; Prov. 1:8-33; John 1:1-3; James 1:22-25 (*see* Commandments, Law, Submission)
Offerings: Luke 21:1-4; Rom. 15:26,27; 1 Cor. 16:1-4; 2 Cor. 9:7 (*see* Giving, Money)

Patience, impatience, toleration: Job 1:20,21; Ps. 40:1-3; 1 Cor. 13:4; James 5:7-11 (*see* Endurance, Steadfastness)
Peace:
    Within: Isa. 26:3,4; Luke 7:50; John 14:27; Phil. 4:4-9 (*see* Quietness, Rest)
    Without: Mic. 4:3,4; Matt. 5:9; Luke 2:14; James 3:17,18 (*see* War)
Pity, compassion, sympathy: Exod. 2:5-10; Col. 3:12-14; 1 Pet. 3:8 (*see* God, Jesus Christ, Merciful)
Pleasure, play: Pss. 16:11; 126:2; Zech. 8:5; Eccles. 3:4 (*see* Happy, Joy, Rejoice, Thanks)
Praise: Ps. 150:1-6; Matt. 21:6-11; Acts 2:46,47; Rev. 19:5; 6 (*see* Joy, Rejoice, Sing Thanks)
Pray, prayer: 2 Chron. 7:13,14; Matt. 6:5-15; 26:36-46
Pride, boasting, conceit, vanity: Prov. 27:1,2; Matt. 23:1-12; Luke 18:9-14; Rom. 12:3,16 (*see* Humility, Self-righteousness)
Promises: Ps. 12:6; Matt. 5:1-12; 6:30-33; Rev. 21:1-4 (*see* Hope)
Providence: Ps. 68:10; Matt. 5:1-12; 28:19,20 (*see* God, Provident)

Quarreling: Prov. 10:12; 17:1; Matt. 12:25; Rom. 12:16; 13:13
Quietness: Eccles. 4:6; Isa. 32:17; 1 Tim. 2:1,2; 1 Pet. 3:3,4

Racism: Ruth 1:15-18; Jon. 4:1-11; John 4:7-10; Col. 3:11
Receive: Matt. 7:7-11; Mark 11:24; John 13:20 (*see* Ask, Pray, Seek)
Redemption: Job 19:25; Ps. 130:7; Rom. 3:21-26; Eph. 1:7,8; Col. 1:11-14 (*see* Jesus Christ: Redeemer, Justification, Salvation)
Regeneration, born again, anew: John 3:1-8; 1 Pet. 1:3,23; Titus 3:5 (*see* Renewal)
Rejoicing: Ps. 118:24; Matt. 5:11,12; John 16:20-22,33 (*see* Joy)
Religion, spirituality: Mic. 6:6-8; Matt. 5:3; John 4:23,24; Gal. 5:16-25; James 1:26,27
Renewal, cleansing: Ps. 51:10-12; Isa. 40:28-31; Rom. 6:3-5; 2 Cor. 4:16 (*see* Regeneration)
Repentance, impenitence: Job 42:5,6; Ps. 51:1-9; Luke 15:11-32
Rest, weary: Jer. 31:25; Matt. 11:28-30; Heb. 4:1-4 (*see* Peace)
Resurrection: John 5:25-29; Rom. 6:5-11; 1 Cor. 15:1-58; 1 Pet. 1:3-9 (*see* Death, Eternal Life, Immortality, Jesus Christ)
Retaliation, vengeance: Matt. 5:38-42; Rom. 12:17-21
Reward: Matt. 5:11,12; 1 Cor. 9:24-27; Phil. 3:12-16 (*see* Sowing)
Righteousness: Amos 5:24; Matt. 5:6,10,20; Luke 18:9-14; Rom. 1:16

Sacrifice: Ps. 51:17; Luke 21:1-4; John 15:13; Rom. 12:1
Safety, security: Ps. 31:23,24; Prov. 29:25; Rom. 8:31-39
Salvation: Luke 19:1-10; John 3:16,17; Rom. 10:9-13; Eph. 2:1-16; 1 Pet. 1:3-9 (*see* God, Jesus Christ, Redemption)

Sanctification: Rom. 6:20-23; 1 Cor. 1:30,31; 1 Thess. 5:23,24 (*see* Holy Spirit)

Scriptures: (*see* Bible)

Second Coming: (*see* Jesus Christ, Judgment Day, Last Things)

Seek, longing: Pss. 34:4-10; 42:1-11; Matt. 7:7-11; Luke 12:28-31 (*see* Ask, Find, Receive)

Self:

    control: 1 Cor. 9:24-27; James 1:19; 2 Pet. 2:5-7 (*see* Discipline, Chastening)

    denial: Matt. 8:20; 19:20; 19:27-29; Mark 8:34 (*see* Sacrifice)

    righteousness: Luke 18:9-14; Rom. 12:3; 2 Cor. 10:17,18 (*see* Humility, Pride)

Sermon on the Mount: Matt. 5:1-7:28

Serve, servant, service:

    God: Josh, 24:24; Matt. 6:24; John 9:4

    Others: Matt. 25:1-30; Mark 9:35; John 13:1-20; 1 Cor. 12:4-11 (*see* Helping, Neighbor)

Sharing: Luke 3:10,11; Acts 4:32; Rom. 15:26,27; Heb. 13:16; 1 John 3:17 (*see* Giving, Money, Offerings)

Sickness: Matt. 6:25-33; Luke 17:11-19; 12:7-10 (*see* Health)

Sin, sinner: Gen. 3:1-24; Isa. 1:16-20; Rom. 6:5-23; Eph. 5:3-10; James 4:17; 1 John 1:8-10 (*see* Evil, Forgiveness, Holiness, God, Jesus Christ, Repentance, Salvation)

Sorrow, bereavement, grief, tears: 2 Sam. 18:31-33; Job 1:20,21; Ps. 30:5; Isa. 61:1; Matt. 5:4; Rom. 8:28; 1 Cor. 15:51-57

Sowing and Reaping: Eccles. 11:1; Matt. 13:3-9; Gal. 6:7-10

Steadfastness: 1 Cor. 16:13; Phil. 4:1; Heb. 10:23-26; James 1:2-4 (*see* Faithfulness, Endurance)

Strength, weakness: Deut. 31:6; Ps. 27:1-14; Isa. 40:28-31; Eph. 3:14-16

Submission, resignation: Job 1:20,21; 42:1-6; Matt. 6:10; 26:36-44 (*see* Obedience)

Suffering: Matt. 26:36-44; Rom. 5:1-5; 2 Cor. 11:23-29; 12:7-10 (*see* Sickness, Sorrow, Trouble)

Sunday, Lord's day, Sabbath: Gen. 2:1-3; Ps. 118:24; Mark 2:23-28

Teach, teacher: Deut. 6:4-9; Matt. 28:20; John 14:26; 2 Tim. 3:14-17

Temptation: Matt. 4:1-11; 6:13; 26:41; 1 Cor. 10:12,13

Thanks, gratitude, thankfulness: Ps. 138:1-8; Matt. 11:25,26; Luke 17:11-19; Acts 28:15

Thanksgiving Day: Pss. 67; 100; 150

Tongue: Prov. 25:11-13; Matt. 12:34-37; Titus 2:7,8; James 3:1-12

Treasures: Matt. 6:19-21; 19:24; Mark 10:17-21; Luke 12:13-21,33, 34

Trinity: Matt. 28:19; John 14:16,17,26; 2 Cor. 13:14; Gal. 4:4-6

Trouble: Nah. 1:7; Isa. 43:1,2; Matt. 5:4; John 14:1,27; 2 Cor. 4:16-5:5 (*see* Need, Sickness, Sorrow, Worry)

Trust, confidence: Ps. 23:1-6; Isa. 12:1,2; 2 Cor. 3:4,5; Heb. 11:1; 13:6 (*see* Believe, Faith, Hope)

Truth: Zech. 8:16; John 8:31,32; 14:6; Phil. 4:8 (*see* Honesty)
Turn, return: Ezek. 18:21,31,32; Zech. 1:3; Matt. 18:3; Acts 3:19
    (*see* Backsliding, Conversion, Renewal, Regeneration)

Understanding: 1 Kings 3:3-9; Prov. 16:16; Mark 12:32-34; Col. 1:
    9,10 (*see* Knowledge)
Unity: John 17:20-26; Rom. 15:5,6; Eph. 4:1-6; Phil. 2:1,2 (*see*
    Cooperation, Harmony)

Victory: 1 Cor. 15:54-57; Phil. 3:12-14; 1 John 5:4 (*see* Reward)

War: Isa. 31:1; Mic. 4:3,4; Matt. 5:9; 26:52 (*see* Peace)
Watch: Matt. 25:1-13; 26:36-46; Mark 13:32-37
Way: Ps. 119:1-16; Matt. 7:13,14; John 14:1-6; 1 Cor. 12:31-13:13
Wealth, riches: Eccles. 2:1-11; Luke 12:13-21; Phil. 4:12; 1 Tim.
    6:17-19 (*see* Giving, Money, Sharing, Treasures)
Willing: Matt. 21:28-31; 26:41; John 9:31; Rom. 7:18-20 (*see*
    Obedient)
Witnessing (includes false): Isa. 6:6-8; Matt. 28:19,20; Mark 1:16-
    20; Acts 13:1-5 (*see* Call, Discipleship, Honesty, Truth)
Woman: Gen. 1:26-31; Prov. 31:10-31; 1 Cor. 11:2-16 (*see* Man)
Word:
    Of God: Ps. 119:105; John 17:17; Heb. 4:12; 1 Pet. 1:25
    Jesus Christ as Word: John 1:1-18; 1 John 1:1-3
    Man and Word: Luke 8:11-15; John 8:51; 14:23,24; 17:6-8 (*see*
        Bible, God, Jesus Christ)
Work, labor, toil: Prov. 6:6-11; Luke 10:38-42; 2 Thess. 3:6-13
Works (good): Matt. 5:16; Rom. 2:6-8; Gal. 2:15,16; James 2:14-26
World, earth:
    Beauty: Job 38:1-41; Eccles. 3:11; Matt. 6:28,29
    Creation: Gen. 1:1-2:3; 2:18-25; Job 33:4; Ps. 24:1,2
    Nature: Pss. 65:9-13; 147:1-20
Worry, anxiety: Ps. 107:1-43; Matt. 6:25-34; John 14:1,2; 1 Pet. 5:7;
    (*see* Peace, Trouble)
Worship: Ps. 95:1-7; Luke 4:16-21; Heb. 12:28 (*see* Prayer, Praise)

Zeal: Prov. 6:6-11; Rom. 12:1; 2 Cor. 9:2 (*see* Serve, Work)